TOURISM: JOURNEY OF HODOPHILES

BASICS OF TRAVEL AND TOURISM

SMITHA S | MTA | M.PHIL | UGC-NET

❧

This book is dedicated to my parents who instilled in me the belief that anything is possible, to my husband who has made everything possible, to all of my well-wishers, and to my amazing students

Contents

I

Basics of Tourism

Introduction

Tourism is such an activity that whole world gets involved in some point of time in some activities or other for rest, relaxation, enjoyment, etc. for satisfied and prosperous life. Knowing the meaning and definition of tourism can help in understanding the dynamics of tourism industry and its interrelations.Tourism has triggered mass movement of people from one country to another. In regard to the meaning and definition of tourism, it varies from country to country and authors to authors.

Difference between Travel and Tourism.

People use travel in synonymous with tourism, though both the terms are not same. The term travel is defined as "The action of moving from one country or place to another". Whereas the term tourism is defined as "The business of providing travel, accommodation, food, entertainment, etc. for tourists" is called as tourism".

Generally, travel signifies the action of individual movement from one location to another or destination by using one or different modes of transportation. It includes different modes of journey undertaken by an individual for leisure, pleasure, employment, study, family/friends, culture, sports/events, health, meeting,education etc. It includes almost all sorts of location and destinations.

On the other hand, Tourism refers to mobility of an individual to places with tourism potential, namely big cities, less trodden places, mountains, beach, national parks, museums, monuments, historical places etc. for leisure or recreational purposes. The mobility is not permanent and non-remunerative in nature. When people travel for tourism, the prime motive for traveling is leisure, recreation and fun. All those activities provide them wonderful and memorable experience that they cherish forever. People travelling with different mindsets and motives do select places of interest taking several factors into consideration. People usually go out for short or long-haul travel. People can travel for countless reasons depending upon their attitude.

Tourism is a growing industry with massive business opportunities. This industry is involved in providing services and facilities to cater to the needs of people while they are on tour. In short, tourism is subset or part of travel. It is a temporary movement outside the usual environment.The main purpose of travel may be anything but it must not be remunerated from the place visited.The movement of individual can be with or without an overnight stay in the place visited. The minimum duration is 24 hours and a maximum duration can be anything, but it differs in conceptual and statistical point of view.

Meaning of Tourism

Etymologically, the word 'tour' is traced or derived from the Latin word 'tornare' and the Greek,'tornos' meaning 'a kind of round wheel' and 'a lathe or circle' respectively. Both words signify the idea a journey or travel circuit. The circle represents here a starting point of trip, which a person ultimately comes back to its beginning or native or place of domicile. A tour describes the nature of journey. This is the act of leaving the starting point and then returning to the original point of trip. So it is a round-trip and the person who takes the journey for one travel motive or several motives may be called as a tourist.

In India the term 'tourism' may be traced back to Sanskrit word 'Paryatan'. It means leaving individual's residence to travel may be for rest or seeking knowledge. There are some related terms in Sanskrit like. 'Deshatan'.Travelling within or different region or country for economic benefits. 'Tirthatan'. Travelling mainly for religious purposes. 'Paryatan'. Travelling for acquiring knowledge.

Definition of Tourism

In 1942, Professors Hunziker and Krapf define tourism as: 'a sum total of relationship and phenomena resulting from travel and stay of non residents, in so far as stay does not lead to permanent residence and is not connected with any permanent or temporary earning activity'.

The Tourism Society (the Institute of Tourism in Britain) in 1976 defines that "Tourism is the temporary short-term movement of people to destinations outside the places where they normally live and work, and activities during their stay at those destinations; it includes movement for all purposes, as well as day visits and excursions

According to Burkart and Medlik (1974) Tourism is deemed to include any activity concerned with the temporary short-term movement of people to destinations outside the places where they normally live and work, and their activities during the stay at these destinations.

In 1993, World Tourism Organization with endorsement by the Statistical Commission of the United Nations defines tourism as: "Tourism comprises the activities of persons travelling to and staying in places outside their usual environment for not more than one consecutive year for leisure, business or other purposes."

In 1994, UNWTO and UNSTAT, with universal acceptance have defined Tourism as "the activities of persons travelling to and staying in places outside their usual environment for less than a year, for any main purpose (leisure, business or other personal purpose) other than to be employed by a resident entity in the country or place visited". This definition has considered three main dimensions on which tourism to be defined and distinguished from different forms of travel:

There are five main characteristics of tourism that may be identified from the UNWTO definition

- Tourism arises from a movement of people to, and their stay in, various destinations.
- · There are two elements in all tourism: the journey to the destination and the stay including activities at the destination.
- · The journey and the stay take place outside the usual place of residence and work, so that tourism gives rise to activities, which are distinct from those of the resident and the working population of the places, through

which the tourist travels and in which they stay.
- · The movement to destinations is of temporary, short-term character, with the intention of returning to the usual environment within a few days, weeks or months.

Destinations are visited for purposes other than taking up permanent residence or employment remunerated from within the places visited.

Concept of Tourism.

Tourism comprises many industries with multiple processes and activities arising from the interaction of tourists with local service providers, community, government and the environment. This industry comprises accommodation, transportation, food services, attraction, entertainment and recreation. The most of tourism definitions have been formed on the basis of the distance traveled the length of stay at the destination and the purpose of visit

A UN Conference on International Travel and Tourism held in Rome in 1963 gave a definition of international tourist as "any person visiting a country other than that in which he has his usual place of residence, for any reason other than following an occupation remunerated from within the country visited". The definition classified tourist and excursionist as visitor.

Tourist is a temporary visitor who stays more than 24 hour and less than one consecutive year in any place.

Excursionist on the other hand, is a visitor who stays for less than 24 hours at a destination.

Traveler - It is a person who is on a trip inside or outside their own living area in a country of residence.

Visitors - Person travelling to a place outside his living area for a period not exceeding one year for purposes except for any remunerative purpose.

Domestic tourist:

Domestic tourists are those person who travels within the country or to a place other than his usual environment or place of residence and stays at hotels or any other commercial accommodation establishments available or in Dharmashalas, Sarai, Musafirkhanas etc. for a minimum duration of not less than 24 hours and maximum length of stay at a time for not more than six months for any of the following purposes

Pleasure (holiday, sports etc.)

Pilgrimage, family and social functions

Business, conferences and meetings

Study and health Domestic Tourist excludes the following persons:

Arriving with motive of taking employment with or without contract to organization or engage in activities remunerated or compensated from within the State/ Union Territories visited.

Coming to establish temporary or permanent residence in State/ Union Territories

Visiting their home town or native place for a short visit with purpose of meeting relations and friends or attending social and religious functions etc. and stay either in their own houses or with friends and relatives.

Foreign tourist:

Foreign tourists are those visitors who hold foreign passports and stay at least twenty four hours in India. The journey should be any one of purposes classified under (i) Leisure (recreation, holiday, pleasure, health, study, religion and sports) (ii) Business, family, friend, mission and meeting.

This excludes the followings:

Persons arriving with motive of taking employment with or without contract to organization or engage in activities compensated or remunerated from within the destination or country visited. Persons coming to establish temporary or permanent residences in India § Persons with Nationality of Nepal entering India through sideways of Indo-Nepal border by land routes. All foreigners entering India through land from Bhutan.Children with less than three years of age , Indians settled abroad and hold Indian passports while on their trip to India, with purpose of recreation, business or other purpose.

Types of Tourism

Tourism has two types and many forms on the bases of the purpose of visit and alternative forms of tourism. Tourism can be categorized as international and domestic tourism.

Tourism has two types and various forms. On the basis of the movement of people tourism categorized into two types. These are following as:

International Tourism

When people visit a foreign country, it is referred to as International Tourism. In order to travel to a foreign country, one needs a valid passport, visa, health documents, foreign exchange, etc.

International tourism further divides into two types; Inbound Tourism & Outbound Tourism.

Inbound Tourism

This refers to tourists of outside origin entering a particular country. When people travel outside their host/native country to another country, then it is called inbound tourism for that country where he/she is traveling. For example when a tourist from Indian origin travels to Japan then it is Inbound tourism for Japan because foreign tourist comes to Japan.

Outbound Tourism

This refers to tourists traveling from the country of their origin to another country. When tourists travel a foreign region than it is outbound tourism for his own country because he/she is going outside their country. For example when a tourist from India travel to Japan then it is outbound tourism for India and Inbound tourism for Japan.

Domestic Tourism

The tourism activity of the people within their own country is known as domestic tourism. Traveling within the same country is easier because it does not require formal travel documents and tedious formalities like compulsory health checks and foreign exchange. In domestic tourism, a traveler generally does not face many language problems or currency exchange issues.

Forms of Tourism

Tourism has various forms on the basis of the purpose of visit and alternative forms. These are further divided into many types according to their nature. Forms of tourism are following as :

Some most important forms of tourism are following as:

Adventure Tourism

Atomic Tourism

Bicycle Tours

Beach Tourism

Cultural Tourism

Ecotourism

Geotourism

Industrial Tourism

Medical Tourism

Religious Tourism

Rural Tourism

Sex Tourism

Space Tourism

Sports Tourism

Sustainable Tourism
Virtual Tourism
War Tourism
Wildlife Tourism

Charecterstatics of Tourism Products

a) Intangible: Tourism is an intangible product means tourism is such kind of product which can not be touched or seen and there is no transfer of ownership, But the facilities are available for specified time and for a specified use. For e.g. a room in the hotel is available for a specified time.

b) Psychological: The main motive to purchase tourism product is to satisfy the psychological need after using the product, by getting experience while interacting with a new environment. And experiences also motivate others to purchase that product.

c) Highly Perishable: Tourism product is highly perishable in nature means one can not store the product for a long time. Production and consumption take place while a tourist is available. If the product remains unused, the chances are lost i.e. if tourists do not purchase it.

A travel agent or tourism operator who sells a tourism product cannot store it. Production can only take place if the customer is actually present. And once consumption begins, it cannot be stopped, interrupted or modified. If the product remains unused, the chances are lost i.e. if tourists do not visit a particular place, the opportunity at that time is lost. It is due to tourism reason that heavy discount is offered by hotels and transport generating organizations during the offseason.

d) Composite Product: Tourist product is a combination of different products. It has not a single entity in itself. In the experience of a visit to a particular place, various service providers contribute like transportation The tourist product cannot be provided by a single enterprise, unlike a manufactured product.

The tourist product covers the complete experience of a visit to a particular place. And many providers contribute to the tourism experience. For instance, airline supplies seats, a hotel provides rooms and restaurants, travel agents make bookings for stay and sightseeing, etc.

e) Unstable Demand: Tourism demand is influenced by seasonal, economic political, and other factors. There are certain times of the year that see greater demand than others. At these times there is a greater strain on services like hotel bookings, employment, and the transport system, etc.

Classification of Tourism

Tourism depending upon size, forms, patterns, and nature can be classified into various types. The criteria wise classifications are outlined as below:

a.On the basis of number of persons ·

Mass Tourism – This is related to the pattern of large number of people travelling to a popular destination over a period of time for recreation and enjoyment. ·

Alternative Tourism – When a person, family or friends visit a newer destination for purposes unique to them and get first-hand knowledge about the destination, it is considered to be alternative tourism

b.On the basis of nationality and pattern of travel

On this basis tourism can be classified into three types, such as; International, National & Internal Tourism. ·

International Tourism - It involves tourists crossing national borders.

It may have two sub types as below.

Outbound Tourism - When a person travels outside his own country for leisure, pleasure or business purposes, his visit is considered to be outbound tourism for his country of residence.

Inbound Tourism - when a country receives residents of another country, they are considered to be inbound tourists. ·

National Tourism - It is the tourism of visitors in any country from within or outside of the economic territory of the country.

Domestic Tourism – When tourism activity takes place only within tourists' own living country. ·

Internal Tourism – Internal tourism comprises of all travels happening within the country including residents' travel (domestic tourism), non-residents' travel within the country (inbound-international tourism).

On the basis of purpose of travel

Business Tourism – When a person goes to attend meeting, conference and exhibition outside from their daily living area. ·

Sports Tourism – It refers to travel which involves either observing or participating in a sports event. · Adventure Tourism – Generally youth likes to go for adventurous tours like trekking, river-rafting and rock climbing.

· Ethnic Tourism– when people travel to different places to know about their own roots, we consider them to be part of ethnic tourism.

On the Basis of Special Interest

As tourists over the years become more selective, such special interest travel has emerged as distinct forms of tourism. These forms of tourism can be explained in marketing terms as niche segments and are alternative forms of mass tourism.

Social Tourism – It is emerging form of special interest tourism for low income group. The weaker section people aim to go to the tour in minimum services without expending their own money or expense very less.

Ecotourism - It involves visiting undisturbed natural areas

5 A's and other Basic Components of Tourism

In tourism components are better known as 5 A's of tourism, i.e. every tourism destination should have attraction, accommodation, activities, accessibility and amenities. Such components are explained below.

· Attraction–Attractions are the pull factors which bring the tourists to travel to the destination. Attractions may be natural resources, man-made built environment, cultural and social features of a destination.

· Accessibility – The facilities and modes of transportation to reach a destination are primary to a tourist destination. Having all other facilities at place, poor accessibility may hinder the success of a destination.

· Accommodation–The facilities of accommodation at a destination are very important as tourists need shelter for rest and night stay while they are on a tour. Varied forms of accommodations are hotels, lodges, resorts, inns, Dharmashalas, campsites, and youth hostels.

· Amenities - Those facilities and services that tourist needs at a destination are considered as amenities. It is vital to the destination for the enhancement of the tourist footfalls.

· Activities –This refers to events, congregations as part of business, sports or social and cultural gatherings such as fairs, festivals or the like. Of late, this segment has become very popular and has emerged as a distinct form of tourism.

· Local residents- Tourism planning starts with an understanding of the need and demand of the locals. As an economic activity tourism should give due priority to the residents of the place.

· Tourist - Tourists are the most important part of the tourism as the customer and end user of services. All procedures and systems are designed in order of the tourist needs and demands. Tourist is only reason of existence of the industry. Revenue for every service provider comes out of the spending of the tourists.

· Infrastructure– It is important to have the basic structures and facilities at the destination for the tourist comfort. Better connectivity, road, electricity, bank, accommodation and restaurant services are some of the examples of tourist infrastructure.

· Information - The success of tourism depends upon the management of information between the guest and service provider.

· Governance–The success of tourism in a country largely depends on the role of public sector in governance. Government plays very important role in the planning and managing tourism activity, which decides the future of the destination.

Typologies of Tourists.

Tourist can be classified as followed on the basis of number of tourist arrivals, motivation behind travel, purpose of travel, and geographical area of the visits

• On the basis of purpose and motivation

· Recreational Tourists - Tourist who goes out from daily living area for relaxation and stress management. · Business Tourist - When a person goes outside from their daily living area for attending meeting, seminar, and conference. · Educational Tourist - Knowledge seekers such as teachers, research scholars and students visiting educational institutions for learning and exchanging knowledge. · Health Tourist - Tourist travels for modern or Ayurvedic treatments to keep themselves healthy. · Religious/Pilgrimage Tourist - Tourist travels for the spiritual or religious purposes.

• On the Basis of Psychographic

The tourists have been classified into three categories by Stanley Plog in 1974 namely

Allocentric, Psycho-centric and Mid-centric.

· Allocentric– A tourist who wishes to explore new places and destinations wish novelty in their trip and wishes to go for adventurous activity.

· Psychocentric– A tourist who wants to go only those types of destination where they have visited before as they are non-adventurous. They like to go to popular and well known places.

· Mid-centric - This category of tourists cover both above motioned type who moves between the both types.

• On the basis of tourist's seeking familiarity or novelty (E. Cohen 1972)

· Drifter- Tourists, who are highly adventurous, make no use of tourist services rather live with local community. ·

Explorers - Tourist, who wants to be independent, travels alone, but uses modern services and seeks comfortable and reliable services, ·

Individual Mass Tourist - Tourists use tourism industry services but not bound to a group and having very less contact with local people, as they have constraints of time as part of fixed itinerary. ·

Organized Mass Tourist - This types of tourist are highly depend on tourism industry for services and they are fully organized, following a tour guide, having very less contact with locals, and they love to stay at their own environment

Significance of Tourism.

Tourism is a very important source of income for many countries. Importance of tourism was placed in the Manila Declaration on World Tourism in1980 as 'an activity essential to the life of nations because of its direct effect on the social, cultural, educational, and economic sectors of national societies and on their international relations. This is in addition to the goods bought by tourists, including souvenirs.

Social Significance –

The social exchange between host and tourist occurs. It helps them to understand one another not only in learning their languages but also their culture. It redefines collective traditional lifestyle, family relationship, community structure, ceremonies and morality.

Economic Significance –

Tourism is one of the most important avenues for revenue generation in developing counties. Tourism provides foreign currency without exporting anything out of the country, helps in regional development,infrastructure development,multiplier effect and growth of GDP

Cultural Significance –

Tourism strengthens culture and it brings positive changes in arts, artefacts, customs, rituals and architecture of the people that occur during the tourism processes, helping reinforcement of culture and traditions.

Environmental Significance

Earning from tourism helps in improved management and planning for environment so that development can be controlled. Tourism spreads awareness about environment problem as it brings tourist closer to the nature which leads to conscious behavior and activities of tourists and host as well to conserve the environment.This type of tourism started before looking after environment benefits and loss.

II
History of Tourism

Introduction

Travel is as old as mankind on the earth. The origin of word travel is seen in its earliest form of *travail*,meaning painful and laborious effort.Food gatherers can be treated as the first travellers.Food gathering stage was followed by production of food and settlements on the river banks.Trade became an important reason in the growth of travel.The invention of wheels , invention of money by Sumerians,cuneiform writing and the concept of inns paved the way for the increasing travel trend and was the sign of beginning of industry,which was later called tourism

Phoenicians were probably the first real business travellers.Egyptians also entertained tourism related activities.In Mediterranean,travel for trade and commerce,religious purposes, medical treatment or education was developed at the early stage.In ancient Greece,people travelled to see the Olympic games in 776 BC.

The rise of Roman empire put an indelible mark in the history of Tourism.At this period,Tourism is considered as a pleasure activity.Romans created excellent networks of road transportation and communication system.Romans created various leisure facilities like space for bath ,resorts,Colosseum for sports and events,trade routes,seaside resorts,summer villas and historical sites were constructed which enhanced the travel propensity of people who want to travel.The emergence of Spas,inns,bars,tour guide,souvenir vendors all marked the development of Tourism during the Roman empire.

The downfall of Roman empire during AD 400 and AD 500 made travel a difficult and boring activity.Between the 5th and 15th century AD,tourism experienced sluggish growth and was referred to as Dark age of Tourism.Tourism was not comfortable due to difficult conditions of roads and highway robbery. Also with the fall of Roman empire came a sharp decline in trade and commerce.

Travel for religious purpose and the adoption and spread of christianity subsequentently led to strong religious bonds.The powerful influence of religions like Christianity,Buddhism,Islam and Hinduism in various parts of the world permit an assimilation and perpetuation of distinctive languages,literature,music,art,architecture and philosophy .Thus Religion played a crucial part in travel.Inns were the forerunners of modern hotels and provide accommodation for spiritual travellers

The religious nature of travel gave way to education,learning and sightseeing and people began to recognize the importance of art,science,culture and education.This period was called the Renaissance.The renaissance marked the next important stage of tourism and the development of full scale urban system and network of roads.By the end of 15th century Italy bacame the object of attraction and was the intellectual capital as well as economic and cultural leader of Europe.Wars were being fought on Italian sol and war played an important played an important part in the dissemination of the Renaissance and the subsequent development of the "Grand Tour".Italy represented both the classical heritage and all the latest ideas and inventions.Young noblemen were being sent abroad to complete their education in France and Italy.The grand Tourist respected the learning,antiquites and social refinements of the old world.The eighteenth century is conventionally considered the golden age of the grand tour.

During this period a great many poets,authors and intellectuals visited Italy and other countries and the grand tourist paved the way for the popular tourism of the nineteenth and twentieth centuries.The introduction of annual holiday which was the forerunner of paid holiday which later was responsible for an extraordinary growth of tourism.The term holidays derives from "holy days" associated with religious observances .The concept of modern annual paid holidays is largely an outcome of the Industrial Revolution.The industrial revolution brought tremondous change in society and this was responsible for the change in the economic and social system.Industrialization also helped in an increase of material wealth and certain improvement in trasport and communication during the second half of the nineteenth and early twentieth century.

The nineteenth century saw the development of large scale pleasure zones and many health resorts were developed to cater the increasing need of healthy people.The introduction of railways in the nineteenth century was yet another crucial landmark in travel history.The birth of organized rail travel came in the year 1841.The man behind this was Thomas Cook.In the early 1870s first class railway travel was introduced by an American,G.M Pullman,who developed pullman coaches.The railways can be considered as one of the most powerful motives for mass travel in 19th century.

Shipping also made significant contribution to travel during the 19th century.The Cunard steam ship company marked an important feature in the growth of North Atlantic shipping.The opening of Suez Canal in 1869 helped the possibility of shortened routes between West and East. Introduction of paid holidays led to greater mobility of the population and helped to develop new industries and also broaden the horizons of millions of people.

The First world war was responsible for a temporary halt to tourist movements.The war was responsible for breaking down international barriers and resulting in the fostering of an ideal,optimistic and peaceful internationalism.Rise in the standard of living of the working and the middle classes in America and European countries was another factor responsible for growth in Tourism.The growth of private car may be identified as a major cause of the decline of the railways.

The role of air transport in the development of international tourism is becoming increasingly important.The world war 1 witnessed the attempts to create commercial airlines.Although international airtravel was born at the end of World war 1 and slowly grew between the two wars,it was only at the end of world war 11 that it made a tremendous breakthrough.The advent of jet travel in1958 was the most dramatic event and brought mass travel to its present form.

In 20th century all the main characteristics of modern tourism were evident in its embryonic form.Changes in mental attitudes towards pleasure seeking,the recognized value of travel for education,an increase in material wealth and improvement in transport,social prestige,the growing need to find relief from working routine-all these factors produced a fertile ground for the development of Tourism.

Evolution and Historical Aspects of Tourism : Early, Medieval and Modern Period

Travel and tourism has a long history which is as old as the civilization itself. The patterns of early age travels were in search of green pastures, food gathering and further religion and business. The instances of travel for special purposes did exist in the early medieval period. Accounts of Marco Polo's world travel, Huensang, & Alberuni's visit to India, Elizabethan travel in Europe are some of the early instances of international travel. During the early period, people with less disposable income mostly travelled for religious purposes and such travels centered on religious places for which basic accommodation such as dharmashalas were created. For traders, Sarai & Inn accommodations were created enroute. However, it was only in religious places in early travel history and trade routes where accommodation units were made available for the overnight stay with food. This was the trend of type of accommodation and churches also funded scholars to travel for learning about religion and culture. Hospitality and tourism are very closely related to each other because of the requirement of accommodation and food . Hospitality industry is one of the segments of the tourism industry which comprises accommodation and food services. Travelers in good old days had no choice to select any room or other services, whereas plenty of options are available for them to select a hotel room.

Early Period of travel.

The historicity of Tourism can be traced to the dawn of the civilisation itself, though the motives and patterns of travel have undergone significant changes over the years. From food gathering to pilgrimage to trade and then for recreation, enjoyment and adventure, travel motivations have evolved over the centuries. Instances of travel for trade during the early Mesopotamia Civilisation are evident. Sumerians invented the wheel and used animals to pull heavy wagons which helped them travel for trade to several places. Sumerians were also the first to build highways for smooth transportation of goods. 'Silk Route' is the well-known highway which extended from East Asia to the West up to the present day Turkmenistan. In the West Asia, people of different countries gathered together to honour the Greek God 'Zeus' at athletic meet after every four year. Greeks were probably the first people who made inns for overnight stay.

Travel during the Medieval Period.

In early history, human beings travelled for food and stayed for a short time, but in medieval time people started travelling to know different cultures and religions. Purpose of the travel was mainly for religious except at rare times for trade. A few wealthy people were funded by the State or churches to travel for educational purposes. In Europe, people were generally funded by churches to travel to holy city of Rome for religious purpose. During this medieval period, some made remarkable journey that brought a revolutionary impact that lasted for centuries. A brief account of some of these prominent travellers is outlined below.

Xuanzang (Huen Tsang). A Chinese traveler who travelled several places in Asia in the seventh century. He recorded all of his travel experiences in his book name 'Journey to the West and India' and 'Great Tsang Records on the Western Region'. At present, these books are important sources to understand the history of the Central Asia and India.

Marco Polo. A traveller from the city of Venice, Italy, Marco Polo started his journey at the age of seventeen with his father and uncle in 1271 A.D. He travelled by following the Silk Route after crossing Armenia, Persia and Afghanistan up to China and came back by sea route. Likewise he travelled second time and completed the circuit for second time. His book "Descriptions of the World" or "The Travels of Marco Polo" is undoubtedly the most influential travelogue about the Silk Route.

Shankaracharya. Popularly known as Adi Shankar traversed length and breadth of the country from south to north, east to west by foot. As a philosopher, intellectual genius, his remarkable journey of the entire country happened before his age of just 32. He established four Peethas or Dhamas or holy places to revitalise the declining Hinduism. Selection of Dhamas in four corners of the country such as; Rameswaram in South in the State of Tamilnadu, Badrinath in the north in the State of Uttarakhand, Dwaraka in the west in Gujarat and Puri in east in the State of Odisha; he advised all Hindus to visit all four Dhamas in a lifetime

Al-Biruni. He was a great scholar of his times who travelled several countries like Greece and India to seek knowledge. Through his travel he wrote books like 'Tarikh Al- Hind' (History of India) after knowing about the religion of India and 'Al-Ustad' (The Master) for the description of early 11th century Renaissance and its Effect on Tourism.

Renaissance was basically a cultural revolution in the Europe during fourteenth to seventeenth centuries AD. It was the time when people of Europe started moving out for learning based on cultural resource and educational reform. The cultural movement brought a powerful cultural movement in Europe. Masses started going out of their homes. Rich travellers used wagons pulled by horses as they kept guns and ammunition for safety. Inns developed by this time by locals alongside the roads to accommodate strangers overnight. Strangers were to share the rooms usually as there was no choice for single room.

Travel remained difficult and dangerous and there were instances of pirates looting the travellers in both roads as well as sea routes. Travel by sea was more dangerous than road. Merchants, soldiers, students and pilgrims' alike used guns, swords and other ammunition for their safety. In Europe governments started issuing pass for the travel inside their territory or country as a licence that is known as visa in modern times. Travellers were of mainly two types as Coltman (1989) mentioned, first was the Elizabethan travellers who travelled for enhancing knowledge and experience. Second was the Pilgrim, who travelled for the religious purposes.

Industrial Revolution and Birth of Mass Tourism.

Industrial revolution made people more comfortable with disposable income at hand. Printing of the currencies made medium of exchange easier. People started having extra money to spend on travel and thus tourism flourished. Industrial revolution started in 1750 A.D and continued up to 1850 A.D. This revolution provided people with more leisure time for travel and tourism as machinery replaced human involvement. Technology had a favorable impact in transportation sector. Modern railways and ships made travelling easy and faster for the people. It expanded the geographies of travel and made travel very cheap and comfortable. Development in transportation along with socioeconomic development of masses helped many to go outside their usual environment. In Europe wealth of middle-class increased and they were also educated which helped in increase in travel demand.

During the period, three or four-week tour was considered as the Grand Tour but many preferred one day trip due to limited income. New forms of tourism and accommodation flourished to cater to the needs of expanding market, spa and seaside resorts became more popular by this time. Attraction so far frequented by only wealthy tourists started getting middle-class tourists. Market structure was continuously going through rapid changes because of the demand for newer destinations.

In Roman Empire famous destinations was Bay of Naples, and Baths. With the fall of Roman Empire, travel to Riviera, the Bay of Naples and Baths came to a halt. The old Roman baths were later used as Spas. The word 'Spa' came from Belgium where a place was famous for its mineral spring. Some famous Spas in the world were Bains-lesBains (France), Lucca (Italy), Baden (Austria) and Bath (England) but in North America people loved to drink spring water and take bath as well for wellness. In Europe seaside bathing became popular in 1800s as people loved to take bath in sea. Gradually, spa and seaside resorts became famous for recreational and entertainment activity with invention of rail which connected these places.

After World War I (1914-18) the rich class of North America influenced the European market. They loved fashion and entertainment which motivated people of Europe to open such places. Naval ships were also used as modern ocean cruise liners. During 1930s 'Paid holiday' became very popular in France and Britain. Tourists from North America and Europe started assembling in Riviera during summer as the rich and middle- class tourists arrived at seaside for getting their skin tanned in the Sun. After World War II (1939-45), the world was in danger for tourism in terms of economic and political situations. It reduced the opportunity of travel overseas and even within the country. This War taught people to understand the importance of industrialization and development in the country. The end of World War II also created new infrastructure for the tourists to fulfill the requirement. The size of middle-class grew very fast during this time and tourism became part and parcel of life for the rich. Thus a huge number of tourists started moving outside for tourism in 1960s and grew continuously till 1980s. This exponential growth in tourism started being called as Mass Tourism.

After the War a huge development in the Air transportation and Communication further helped tourists to go out for a longer distance. In nineteen centuries industrial workers were working for six days in a week to earn livelihood sufficient enough sustain daily needs. They did not have sufficient money to travel but industrial revolution and the evolution of trade unions and also evolution of democratic forms of government brought changes in the society. Workers were provided annual paid holidays to go out for leisure. Middle-class had sufficient disposable income to spend on tourism activities. Increase in travel during this time was only because of the availability of facilities like transportation and varied places of interests. Development in the technology of transportation also led to the increase in the movement of people. Both the rich and middle-class could travel in the same train.

Evolution and Development of Transport. In the past people were unable to travel long distances as they had to walk but the invention of the wheel made journeys easy. Use of cart with the help of pet animals to pull it, increased efficiency as animals could take more load and also reduced the travel time. Horses and oxen were common animals used in pulling carts which helped people to find new places of interest

Road Transport.

As per the historical evidences, the first roads were constructed by the Mesopotamians. Stagecoaches were first made in Hungary in fifteen century A.D. and started regular services. Henry Ford introduced famous automobile name Model T in 1908 A.D. The first good road network was constructed in 1920 in USA. In twentieth century, railway and steamships were considered as very popular modes of transportation. Availability of car and coaches helped in reaching destinations in quick time. However, these were not preferred for long-haul transfers. Later national and international highways were built in the North America and Europe which helped rapid growth in road traffic. Large highway construction also made long haul travel popular. In 1930, Germany became the leader in the development of motorways.

Railways.

Rail travel became comfortable and economic mode of transportation just after its introduction. It was introduced in England in 1825 and started regular services five years later. First train was run between Manchester and Liverpool. Railway track was built in US in between 1826 to 1840 which is known as first railway track in the world. The introduction of train made travel easy and safe for the tourists and affordable for middle-class to travel both long and short route journey. The father of modern travel trade Thomas Cook organized a train tour from Leicester to Loughborough in England in 1841. France got its first railway in 1863 and very soon expanded up to Monte Carlo in Monaco. Thus a gambling casino was built in 1868 that became very popular instantly in a short time. More and more railway systems in different parts of the world are experimenting with newer concepts.The French manufactured TGV (Trains a Grande Vitesse)began its commercial operation in September 1981 between Paris and Lyon in France.

Air Transport.

Deutsche Lufthansa started first ever flight in Germany in 1903 on Berlin – Leipzig Weimar route. Charles A. Levine was the first international and transatlantic passenger travelled between New York to Germany on 7 June

1927. In 1926, the first US airline Launched with the name of Varney Airlines but operated after 11 days when Western airline started services on 17 April 1926. The first mile carried flight run between Florida to Havana, Cuba in on 28 October 1927 and also took the same passenger on same route on 16 January 1928. But air travel was popularized by airline DC-3 and Boeing 314 a Transoceanic Clipper. BritishFrench joint venture product named Concord was the first high speed aircraft and was developed in 1967 and its first flight started in 1969. In India air services started with the efforts of J.R.D. Tata before independence of India. Immediately after the independence, Indian government took over Tata Airlines to provide domestic and International air services. Tata Airlines were founded in 1932 and the name was changed to Air India and Indian Airlines after the takeover by the government.

Water Transport

It is evident from the historical findings that first dockyard was found in Lothal Gujarat, India. The evidences revealed that ship building was known to Indians as early as 2400 B.C. But the Phoenicians are considered to be pioneers in the ship making activities. They purchased spice and perfume from the east and lines and papyrus from Egypt. Greek became the next sea hitters after Phoenicians. Many sea hitters traveled round the world and found sea route to different places during the medieval period. America's sea route was discovered by Christopher Columbus and he is also credited with having named West Indies. Portuguese were also the great sailors. India's sea route was discovered by Vasco Da Gama in 1498 as he reached India at Calicut in Kerala in the West Coast. Water transport was first introduced in England in 1772, which was an organized transport system. In Clyde, Avon and Thames rivers services of steamboat were popularized in 1815.

Evolution of the Hospitality services.

In India, sarais and dharamshala were made for the travellers and pilgrims in the olden days for providing room and food services. Evidences support that the Emperor Ashok made several accommodation facilities for Buddhist monks. In early years, temple priests were also the providers of accommodation services to the pilgrims and 'yatris'. In Europe travellers were provided inn as eating and sleeping point. Rooms were also provided by the churches with food and other facilities. The term 'inn' was derived from the Hebrew word 'malon' and it was also called 'kataluma' in Greek. Innkeeper realising its importance made large inns with big dormitories where travellers could stay in large numbers. The emergence of travel for the purpose of trade started in fifteenth century. Travellers who travelled for the purpose of trade and commerce needed to stay during long distance travel. Demand for quality services and safety was the priority of the travellers. In eighteenth century, travellers started using private coaches for travel and concept of toll gates were raised for the maintenance of roads and bridges. Development of overnight stay changed the concepts of accommodation. Big accommodation operators joined together in providing better services with good dining and parking facility. Not only accommodation units were increased near such stations but also other services started being popular there too got increased. The demand for more facilities resulted in big accommodation units opening in the heart of cities to cater to the needs of the travellers.

Tourism and development are very close to each other as both are benefited mutually each other. Such close relation can indicate the requirement of accommodation and food services at the transit and destination localities. Tourism in varied scale and types has existed since human existence. People always love to go new places for recreation, food, enjoyment and adventure. In early history, human travelled mostly for food, but people started travelling to learn about the culture and religion during medieval time. During this time, most of the travels were undertaken for religious purpose. There are some famous travelers such as; Al-Biruni, Marco Polo, Shankaracharya and Xuanzang (Huen Tsang) who created the history through their travel and travel accounts. In India, Sarais and Dharamshala were made for the travelers and pilgrims in olden days for providing room and food services

Summary

Travel was originally inspired by the need for surviving (food, shelter, and security), the desire to expand trade and quest to conquer. As the transportation system improved the curiosity for transforming the vast and virgin world into a close neighbourhood created a new industry i.e. Travel and Tourism. Christian missionaries, Buddhist monks and other traveled far and wide carrying religious messages and returned with fantastic images and opinions about alien people.

For centuries movement of people continued to grow due to the efficiency of transport tand the assistance and safety which the people could travel. By the end of the 15th century, Italy had become the intellectual and cultural center of Europe. It represented the classical heritage both for the intelligentsia and the aristocracy.

During the 16th Century, travel come to be considered as an essential part of the education of every young Englishman. Travel thus became a mean of self – development, and education in its broadest sense. The educational travel was known as **'Grand Tour'.**

The industrial revolution brought about significant changes in the pattern and structure of British society. Thus, the economy of Britain was greatly responsible for the beginning of modern tourism. It also created a large and prosperous middle class and because of great improvement in transportation systems in latter half of the 18th century and the first quarter of the 19th century, an increasing number of people began to travel for pleasure.

However, the developments of rails, roads, steamships, automobiles, and airplanes helped to spread technology across the globe. Earlier travel was a privilege only for wealthy people but with the industrial revolution, the scenario altogether changed. Transportation, as well as accommodation, became affordable to middle and working-class citizens.

Essentially, with the development of jet travel, communication, new technology, tourism, and travel became the world's largest and fastest growing industry.

III

Principles of Tourism

Leiper's Tourism system model (1990):

Neil Leiper suggested a model on Tourism System in 1979 (further updated in 1990).Leiper outlined three geographical elements in his model :Human Elements, Tourist, Geographical Elements .

Travellers generating region - This is a place from where a trip starts and ends. · Tourist destination region - This is the target place where tourist visits · Transit route - This is an area where tourist travels, stays and exchanges transportation mode. Industrial Elements · All services en-route to, within and on return from the destination. · Including logistics, accommodation and all other tourism services.

TOURISM SYSTEM

Leiper (1979) developed the whole tourism systems based on the systems theory and identified five basic components: Tourists, generating regions, transit routes, destination regions, and a tourist industry operating within physical, cultural, social, economic, political, and technological environments. He conceptualized tourism as an open system.

The following are the four components embedded in the Leiper's model. I. The Human Component: · The Tourist II. The Geographical Component: · The Generating Region · Transit Route Region · The Destination Region III. The Industrial Component IV. The Environmental Component

Leiper proposed six aspects within the model which are interrelated, interdependent and interact with each other and function as a group while responding to the external influences. Thus it is an open system where influences are found within the system as well as external to the system. The human component consists of the tourists, the geographical component consists of traveler-generating regions, transit route regions and tourist-destination regions, the industrial component involving the various business and organizations that provide services and finally, the environmental component comprising of the social, technological, legal and ecological aspects. All these aspects weave together as a whole tourism system in a structural manner

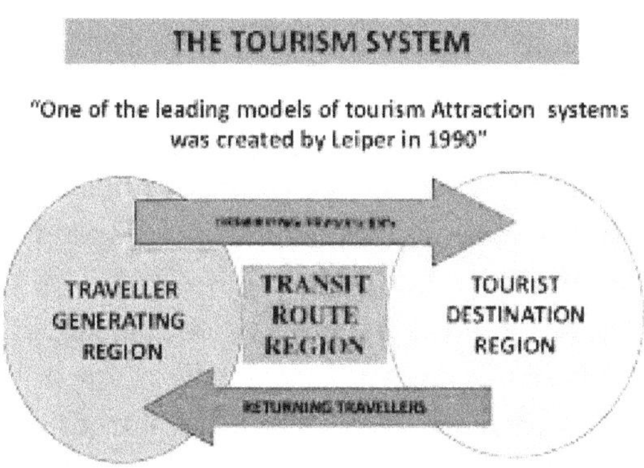

Fig.1-Leiper's Model of Tourism System

The human component consists of the tourists, the geographical component consists of traveler-generating regions, transit route regions and tourist-destination regions, the industrial component involving the various business and organizations that provide services and finally, the environmental component comprising of the social, technological, legal and ecological aspects.

All these aspects weave together as a whole tourism system in a structural manner. Figure-1 provides the pictorial representation of the Leiper's model of the components of the tourism system.

The Human Component

The human component specified in the model is the tourists who undertake tourism to a destination of their interests. A tourist is a person who traverses away from his place of residence to another place for a short span of stay with an aim to spend his holidays.

A person can be called as a tourist if he stays for at least 24 hours and not more than one year in a destination either within the country or outside the country of residence not involving in any remunerative activity. Tourism, according to the Oxford dictionary, is "the theory and practice of touring or travelling for pleasure".

Tourists undertake different forms of tourism as per their need like recreation, pleasure, business, education, health, pilgrimage, culture and they are called as recreational tourists, pleasure tourists, business tourists, education tourists, health tourists, pilgrimage tourists and cultural tourists in that order.

It is based on the motivational push that tourists undertake their trip to a particular destination. It all happens with the available forms of tourism. Therefore, it completely depends on the purposes of travel.

As per the definition of UNWTO's (United Nations World Tourism Organization), "tourism comprises the activities of persons travelling to and staying in places outside their usual environment for not more than one consecutive year for leisure, business, and other purposes". It is clear from the definition that tourists are temporary residents of the destination of visit.

After touring, they return to their original place of residence or their place of departure. According to Leiper (1979), the fundamentals of tourism are traced back to Greek origins, likened to a circle, reflecting a key component of tourism and returning to the point of departure.

The Geographic Component.

The geographic component refers to the geographical area involved in the tourism process. Tourists depart from a geographical area – the place of origin, utilize a geographical route and reach a geographical area – the place of arrival or destination of visit.

Similarly, they reach their area of origin after completion of the trip taking a complete cycle of the geographical components. Thus, there are three geographical areas involved in the conduct of tourism.

The geographic components comprise of the following three aspects:

1. Tourist Generating Region(TGR)
2. Travel Route Region(TRR) and
3. Tourist Destination Region(TDR)

Tourism Generating Regions (TGR).

Tourism Generating Region refers to the place where the tourist starts and ends his tour. It is the location of permanent residence from where he departs for tour and reaches after completion of trip. It is also referred to the source region of journey as well as the geographical area of demand. According to Dann (1977), it is the geographical setting pertaining to the motivational and behavioral pattern termed as "Push" factors.

'Push' factors are the intangible wishes or desires arising in the minds of a person. These are influenced by the social, psychological, and economic forces generated from within the person.

The aspects like mundane environment, exploration, self-evaluation, relaxation, prestige, family relations, and social interaction are found within the minds of the people of the tourist-generating region. These pertain to the psychological push factors. Influence of family, reference groups, social classes, culture, and sub-cultures are the factors pertaining to the social push factors.

The demographic aspects like age, sex, educational qualification, income and marital status also contribute to the push factors. The economic push factors are the disposable income added with the available leisure time joint together that play vital role in the tourist-generating region.

Apart from the above mentioned factors in the tourist generating region, the aspects like ticketing services, tour operators, travel agents and marketing and promotional activities present in the departure area play a major role as push components.

Transit Route Region (TRR).

Transit route refers to the path throughout the region across which the tourist travels to reach his or her destination. It is the path that links the tourist generating regions and the tourist destination regions, along which the tourists travel.

When the tourists undertake a long haul, travel it is necessary to take a temporary stoppage called a transit route. The transit route includes stopover points, which might be used for convenience of the tourist or due to the presence of various attractions throughout the travel route that can be visited by the tourists.

The transit route enables the tourists to change flight or stop for some time for refueling. The transit route might differ from the start of the travel from the generating region and ending of the travel from the destination region.

The transit route may be crossed with the different types of transportation like air transport or rail transport or water transport or road transport or a combination of all these types of transports according to the necessity of the tourist. Thus, the transit rout region is a vital component in the tourism system.

Tourist Destination Region (TDR).

Tourist Destination Region refers to the destination, which the tourists prefer to visit during their travel. It is the location, which attracts tourists for their temporary stay. The destination region is the core component of tourism, as it is the region, which the tourist chooses to visit, and which the core element of tourism is based on. It is the supply side of the tourism products that pull the tourists.

This component includes the natural attractions, cultural attraction, and various entertainment factors, accommodation, facilities, services, amenities, safety and security available in the destination of visit that ultimately pull the tourists. The new age tourists mostly demand now-a-days special interest tourism products available in the destination region.

The qualitative aspects that are absent or lacking in the tourist-generating region and available in the tourist destination region form as the basic attractions that pull the tourists towards TDR. The location has the attributes as anticipated by the tourists that retains loyal tourists from the generating regions.

The Industrial Component

The next important component in the Lieper's model is the industry. Industrial component refers to the businesses and organizations that promote tourism related products. These firms thrive to cater to the needs and wants of the tourists.They impart full-fledged products and services to the tourists through attractions, accommodation, accessibility and amenities.

It is a composition of many small firms that provide tourist attractions and services to the tourists in an affordable manner. Tourism industry is not an individual entity and all the industrial components of the tourism industry function together as an amalgam as tourism cannot function in the absence of even a single aspect of the industrial component. Tourism industry is a mixture of many industries. They are:

- Tourist Services Industry
- Accommodation Industry
- Transport Industry
- Entertainment Industry
- Tourist Attraction Industry

Doxey's Irritation Index 1975

This theory describes about the situation how a guest and host interact with gradual development of tourism at a destination. ·

- Euphoria –During the initial phase residents welcome tourists as guest. Residents treat them with high esteem.
- Apathy – When residents lose interest in tourism and relation with tourists becomes more formal. ·
- Annoyance – Saturation in the approach of host for the tourists as the host have doubt about the tourist activities.
- Antagonism – Open expression of irritation for the tourist. Tourists are not welcome at the destination

Butler's Tourist Area Life Cycle (1980)

Tourist Area Life Cycle (TALC) is a model developed by Butler (1980) to show how a destination goes through various stages from starting (exploration) to end (Decline/rejuvenation).

Tourism Area Lifecycle Model ·

Exploration - New location, small number of tourists, adventurous travel.

·

Involvement - If tourists are accepted by local, some involvement in tourism infrastructure begins. · Development - Huge investment takes place in the destination by outside investors in infrastructure development. ·

Consolidation - When growth rate is very high in the area with the involvement of tourism professionals.

· Stagnation–When there is no scope for future growth, destination is already flooded with service providers, and destination seems to be crowded. ·

Decline/Rejuvenation - The popularity of the area decreases. Outsiders move out and only local residents take care of tourists, where day trippers (excursionists) become the main source of income. Rejuvenation of the place takes place when it attracts different people with modernized services.

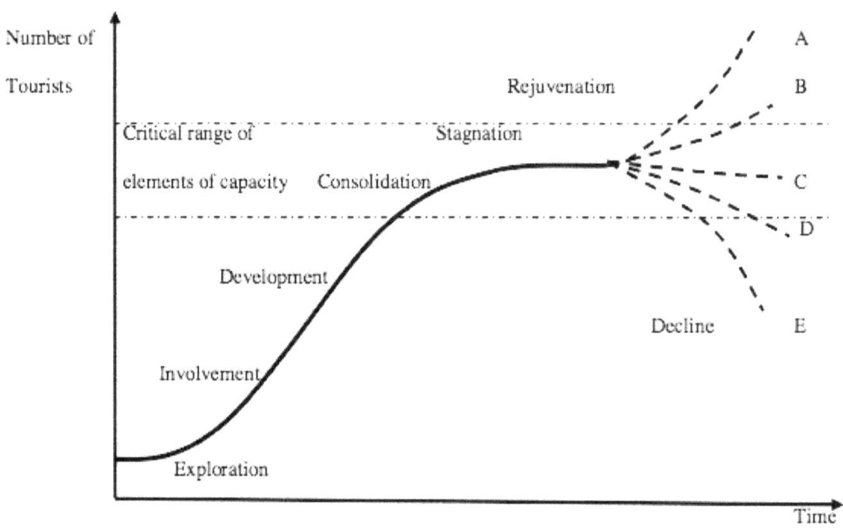

Tourism Area Lifecycle concept by Butler

Motivation

According to Stephen P. Robbins "motivation is the willingness to exert high levels of efforts toward organizational goals, conditioned by the effort ability to satisfy some individual need".. Motivation can also be defined as one's direction to behavior, or what causes a person to want to repeat a behavior or drop a behaviour. Motivation is a willingness, desire to do a particular activity. It does not require any logic or reason; only desire or willingness to perform a task is important.

Motivation and Purpose of Trip Motivation and purpose of trip are closely related. UNWTO definition of tourism broadly categorized travel purpose as business travel, leisure travel and miscellaneous travel. It includes travel to visit friends and relatives (VFR), health and religious travel. Tourists traveling for above mention three purposes are three types of travel motivation. It is important to know needs and desire of tourist, as it reflects the motivation for travel to a particular destination for fulfillment of their internal desire.

Types of Motivation

Motivation can be classified into categories:

Intrinsic Motivation: It refers to the individual's stimuli which comes from inside through the core of the heart or mind of an individual, for performing a specific task. Intrinsic motivation does not includes those activities that are done for the sake of an external reward.

Extrinsic Motivation: It refers to the individual's stimuli which comes from outside attraction. It involves executing an action influenced by the outer stimuli, to attain an external reinforcements or rewards from others such as money, praise, status etc.

Maslow's Need Hierarchy Theory

According to Maslow, individuals must fulfill the needs at the lower levels to be further motivated to the next levels. In 1943 Abraham Maslow proposed a theory named by Need Hierarchy Theory of Motivation.As per his theory a human desire will sequentially follow the five stages of needs and after that need ends. Needs has been arranged in such a way of hierarchy, starting from the lowest need physiological to safety, love (social), esteem (ego), and finally, self-actualization.

Physiological: The need for survival is most basic need for every individuals i.e. for food, water, and shelter including hunger, thirst, sex and other physiological needs. Safety: Safety ugs the feeling an individual get when they are physically, mentally, or emotionally secure or have low fears and anxieties.

Social: After having satisfied with their physiological and safety needs individual need or seek for love and belonging including affection, acceptance and friendship. These needs can only be met through satisfactory relationships or acceptance by others such as with family members, friends, classmates and other peoples.

Esteem: After being satisfactorily met their lower needs, individual begin to develop positive outlooks of self-worth and self-esteem. The individual feel pride in their work and self. Esteem is classified as Internal esteem - as self-respect, autonomy and achievement. External esteem- as status, recognition and attention.

Self- Actualization: It is to realize and nurture talents into the full potential and capacities or the drive to become what an individual is capable of becoming.

Travel Motivation Motivation is an intrinsic property of a human-being that arises from the inside or of psychological origin. Tourism is an activity that is driven by the motivational forces i.e. a combination of internal and external forces.

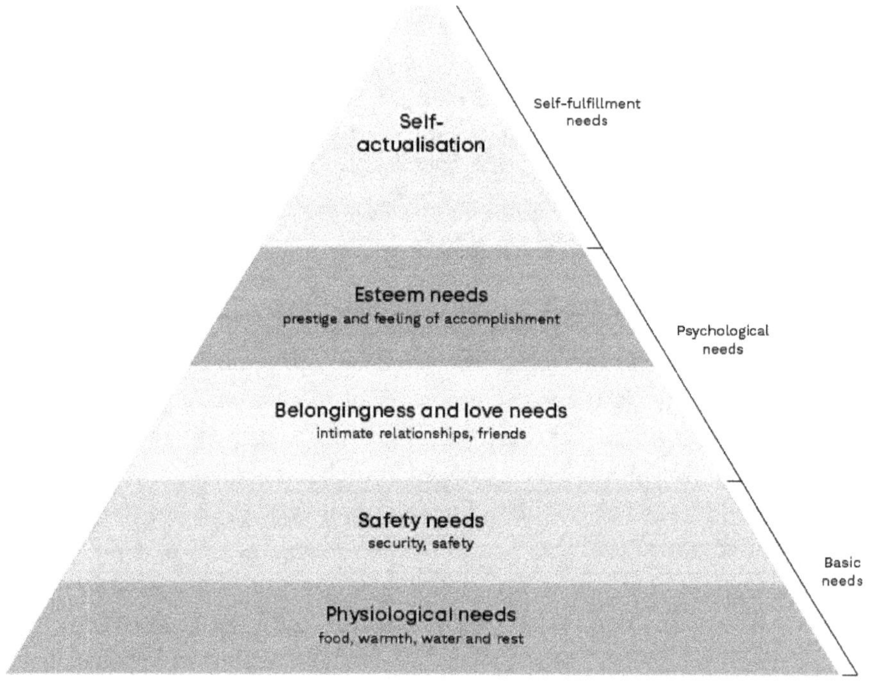

Maslow's Need Hierarchy Theory

There are some common factors influencing tourist travel decisions such as · Availability free time · Disposable income · Age and status · Attractiveness of destinations

Gray's Travel-Motivation Theory.

Gray explains the motivation of individual go to natural settings and given two motives for travel:

Wanderlust: It describes the motive or the desire to go from a known to an unknown place. It is travelling from or leaving a familiar places to go and see different or unfamiliar places. It is about going to different destinations to experience monumental and socio-cultural heritage.

Sunlust :It is a type of travel to a destination that can provide the tourist with specific facilities or better amenities. It is travelling for particular purpose or facilities that are not available in place of residence of the tourist.

Plog's Classification

The tourists have been classified into three categories by Stanley Plog in 1974 namely

Allocentric, Psycho-centric and Mid-centric.

· Allocentric– A tourist who wishes to explore new places and destinations wish novelty in their trip and wishes to go for adventurous activity.

· Psychocentric– A tourist who wants to go only those types of destination where they have visited before as they are non-adventurous. They like to go to popular and well known places.

· Mid-centric - This category of tourists cover both above motioned type who moves between the both types.

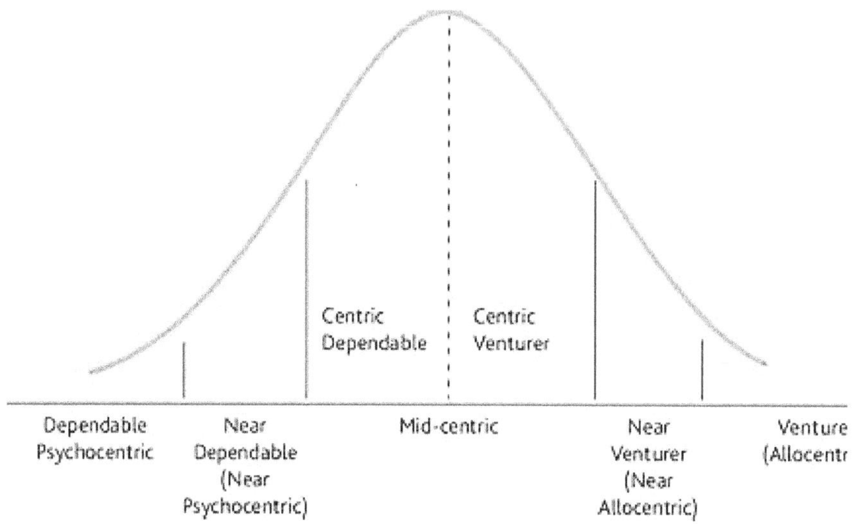

Plog's Classification

McIntosh and Goeldner Categorization of Travel Motivation

McIntosh has stated that basic travel motivators may be grouped into four broad categories:

Physical Motivators These types of motivation are concerned with the individual physical health and well-being involves physical relaxation and rest, sporting activities, medical care or treatment and specific remedial health management. It include physical motivators that are concern with health from recreation to attending yoga camp to medical treatment for upkeep of health.

Interpersonal Motivators Human are social animal and always keen to make new friends, have a desire to visit and meet relatives and friends, or simply want to escape from the daily hassles of everyday life. These type of motivators are termed as interpersonal motivators.

Cultural Motivators Cultural motivators are describe as curiosity that tourists have and want to experience different people's cultures and lifestyle. These are related with tourists desire to travel to different destination, in order to know about other countries, people, their culture, tradition, life style, art, music etc.

Status and Prestige Motivators Tourists travel to secure respect among their friends or in family and recognition of education and knowledge or for pursuit of hobbies. These types of motivators are identified with the need for fame and status or of personal esteem and personal development. It also include travel for business or professional interests.

Push Factors.

Push factors are defined intrinsic drives or desire that motivate people to travel. Push factors are initiating travel desire of an individual to engage in recreational activities or tourism. It is internal motives that drive tourists to seek activities for their needs fulfillment. It is the internal psychological imbalances that pushes or forces the individual to search for optimal level of motivation to travel. Some push factors of travelling are: · Exploration and evaluation of self. · Escape from a perceived mundane environment. · Relaxation. · Health and fitness. · Re-experiencing family. · Facilitation of social interaction. · Enhancement of kinship relationships. · Novelty. · Cultural experiences. · Education. · Prestige.

Pull Factors

Pull factors are extrinsic motivations that pulls an individual towards the product offerings of the destination and destination itself. Pull factors appear due to the attractiveness and the attributes associated with the destination. It is related to the external condition, cognitive aspects or choices available on a destination such as attractions, climate, culture etc. Pull factors are usually destination specific, it is the destination setting or characteristics itself that attract several tourists. Pull factors are more identifiable and can be compared between destinations according to the knowledge and information that tourists gathered about a destination.

Tourism is a people- centric and one of the fastest growing industries industry. Assessing behaviour and motivations of tourist is a critical task as travel decisions of tourist depends on it. There has always being some forces behind travel decisions. It is some type of motivation that impulse people for movement from one place to another. A motive is anything which prompts the person to act in a certain way, or develop an inclination for specific behavior. Motive can be defined as an inner state of our mind that activates and directs human to act. It is an intrinsic to us and is exhibit by our external behavior. Travel satisfy both lower and higher levels of needs, such as physiological, psychological or biological needs that direct individual's behavior and activity. It is a willingness, desire to do a particular activity.

It includes travel to visit friends and relatives (VFR), health and religious travel.

Tourism Demand

According to Song et al. 2010, "Demand is made of all those travelling to some place (tourists and destination). It can be measured by taking into account four elements: people (tourists), money (expenditure, receipts), time (stays and travels durations) and space (distances, lengths of trips).

According to Cooper et al, 1993, Tourism demand is, "The total number of persons, who travel or wish to travel and use tourist facilities and services at places away from their places of work or residence."

According to Professor H.P. Gray, Tourism demand can be discussed under two sub-parts as: Wanderlust: The desire to exchange the known for the unknown, to leave familiar things and to seek new experiences, places, people and cultures. Sunlust: A desire to travel and enjoy sunny places.

Tourism demand

Tourism demand may be defined as requirement of various tourism products (Goods and services) at a particular place or market in a given time period at a given price. More precisely, demand of tourism products is called as tourism demand. It involves demand of tour packages, tour components and variety of services like escort and guide services, catering services and foreign currency exchange etc.

Types of tourism demand:

Tourism demand is of following types depending upon its existence: 1) Active demand. 2) Potential demand. 3) Deferred demand. 4) Suppressed demand. 5) Future demand. 6) Creative demand.

Various types of tourism demand can be further understood as follows:

1) Active demand: It refers to total number of people, who are actually utilizing Tourism Demand and Supply different tourism products in current time at a particular place / market.

2) Potential demand: It refers to total number of people, who are currently not utilising any tourism product but may utilise or undergo any tour in near future at a particular place /market.

3) Deferred demand: It refers to all those individuals, who have potential to undergo any tour but they have delayed their plan due to some reasons. These reasons may be lack of leisure / free time, health issue or any family problem etc.

4) Suppressed demand: It refers to all those people, who can undergo tours but are not utilising any tourism product because of lack of motivation and sufficient information. This demand can be converted into active demand through variety of motivational efforts.

Factors affecting demand in tourism:

Different factors like psychology, economic condition, technology and geography affect tourism demand at large. These may be discussed as follows:

Socio-economic factors: These factors include income, purchasing power, disposable income, standards of living, economic status, paid holidays availability, organisational incentives. Competitive prices of tourism products, increase in leisure time, and demographic structure of population (Gender, age, religion, affiliation and type of family) also affect tourism demand.

Psychological factors: These factors include personal motives, personal attributes / perceptions / biases, awareness, education, personality type and physiological well-being etc.

Technological factors: These factors include mobile phones, TV's, computer with internet, electronic displays, mobile apps like Yatra.com, Goibibo, oyo rooms and make my trip etc.

Geographical factors: These factors include geographic location of destination, landscapes, snowy peaks, rivers, climate, seasons and natural hazards etc. Factors at destination: It includes development level, quality of product, tourist / travel formalities, tourism policy of the destination, creative tourism trends, destination image and branding etc.

Indicators of tourism demand

Travel propensity is the most widely used indicator for Tourism Demand.

Indicators of tourism demand –

1) Economic indicators: The financial status of people in a market is a major indicator of tourism demand. If the economic condition of people in a market is in growing phase then the demand for tourism products will increase most probably. On the other hand, if the economic condition of people in a market is poor, then the demand for tourism products will decrease at large.The economic indicators are:Employment of people, ,Income of people, Local entrepreneurship in a market,Local investment in different venture

2) Socio-cultural indicators: There are certain social factors that affect the movement of local people for tourism activities. However, the social

effect may be positive or negative depending upon multiple aspects (Financial structure of people, lifestyles etc.). The cultural factors that involve exploration and provide ample space for creativity enhance local movement to new places, thereby increase the tourism demand.

3) Psychological indicators: Psychological aspects of people at any place / market constitute tourism demand in a given time. Educated and motivated people indicate increase in tourism demand and contrary to this less educated and least motivated people indicate decrease in tourism demand.

Various psychological indicators are: Awareness level of people for tourism activities. Motivational atmosphere for tourism activities. Family structure and support. Marital status. Working environment. Social status.

4) Geographical indicators: Geography of any place / market also indicates demand for tourism products. The places that are well connected through variety of modes of transportation and are easily accessible, generally receive better services and are up to date with current tourism trends. Thus, such places show an effective demand for tourism.

Various geographical indicators are: Terrain of place / market (Plain region, mountain region, desert or coastal region). Ease of accessibility up to or within the place / market. Distance of the place from a bigger market,Concept and Impacts of Tourism Availability of multiple modes of transportation (Roadways, railways, airways and waterways).

5) Climatic indicators: Climate of any place or market is also an important indicator of tourism demand. The place having better climatic conditions shall lead towards better inflow of tourists to the place and least outflow of people to other destinations, thereby decreasing the demand of local people for tourism products.

. Various climatic indicators are: Seasons (Summer, winter, monsoon and spring season). Calamities like cloudbursts, hot winds, landslides and floods etc.

6) Technological indicators: Technological development of a place / market is important indicator of demand for tourism products. Technological empowerment of local people helps them to utilise available tourism products and new tourism trends in the market, thereby increasing the tourism demand. Contrary to this, lack of technological support, prohibit people from availing tourism products, thereby leading towards decrease in demand for tourism products.

Various technological indicators are: Availability of smart mobile phones. Availability of internet facility. Availability of mobile applications.

Availability of online service providers like MMT, YATRA, OYO rooms, Go ibibo, Taj hotels, Oberoi hotels, Indigo airlines, Air India etc.

Determinanats of Tourism Demand

The two main determinanats of Tourism demand are personnel view factors and world view factors

Personnel View factors are of two types

a.Lifestyle factors include employment,disposible income,working women ,mobility etc

b.Life cycle factors include age ,family size,race and gender

World view factors are level of urbanization,social,cultural,technological , political factors etc

Importance of Statistical Measurement in Tourism

- For evaluating the magnitude and significance of Tourism
- For planning and development of physical facilities
- For marketing and promotion
- To know about the changes in tourist fashion

Measuring Tourism Demand

Statistics of tourism demand:

While measuring tourism demand, following three aspects are taken into consideration.

These are: 1) Volume statistics. 2) Value statistics. 3) Visitor profile statistics.

1) Volume statistics refers to following aspects: Total number of individual tourist arrivals and the total number of tourist departures.

It is added by following equilibriums: – No. of trips= (No. of individuals) (Number of trips per individual) – Total tourist nights= (No. of trips) (Average length of stay) Arrival in accommodation establishment. Business trip. Country of residence. Domestic tourist. Inbound tourist. Outbound tourist. International tourist. Duration of trip.

2) Value statistics:

Value statistics while measuring tourism demand includes following: Measurement of economic value of foreign visitors and outgoing visitors (expenditure). International tourism expenditure. International tourism receipts. Leisure trip.

3) Visitor profile statistics: Visitor profile includes following details: Visitor name. Age. Sex. Group type. Occupation. Income level. Origin and

destination. Mode of transportation. Purpose of visit. Length of stay. Accommodation used. Activities. Tour package / independent travel.

While measuring tourism demand, following broad spectrum are taken into consideration: D= f (Propensity, resistance) In which D stands for tourism demand. Propensity = Person's predisposition to travel = How willing is the person to travel. = What types of travel experiences he / she prefer. Resistance= Relative attractiveness of various destinations. =Economic crunches (Time and cost involved in travelling). =Cultural distance-extent of cultural differences. = Cost of services. =Quality of service. =Seasonality.

Travel propensity is effective measure of tourism demand. It is further of two types as net travel propensity and gross travel propensity. Net travel propensity refers to the percentage of population that has taken at least one trip in a year or given time.

. The travel propensity is measured as:

1) Net Travel Propensity: Net travel propensity refers to the percentage of population that has taken at least one trip in a year or given time.

2) Gross Travel Propensity: Gross travel propensity refers to average number of trips undertaken by people in a year or given time.

3) Travel Frequency: It is the ratio of gross travel propensity to net travel propensity. Based upon, various factors, determinants and available feedback from market, the tourism demand at a particular place / market in a given time frame can be calculated more accurately and effectively

Problems of Measurement

The tourist statistics is mostly concerned with arrivals and departures and more particularly with the arrivals.There are many difficulties in the matter of counting.Due to double counting,the absolute figures of tourists visiting almost every country tend to be inflated.Another problem of statistical measurement in Tourism arises from the difficulty of differenciating between tourist and other travellers.At various destinations,it becomes difficult to distinguish between tourist and the residents and the working population.Tourist normally use public transport or own private transport at various destinations without stopping and often without registering their arrival.At the destinations,tourist use a variety of accommodation ranging from hotels to friends and relatives homes.They eat in the same catering establishments and buy items for use and other services from the same source from which these are bought by those who are not tourists.

These general problems of statistical measurement are encountered in countries having common borders.It is in these countries like Europe,Middle East,South America and South-East Asia encounter such problems of measurement

Tourism Satellite Account

The Tourism Satellite Account (TSA) is a new framework adopted by the United Nations Statistical Commission that provides an important platform towards forging improved understanding of the structure and role of tourism in the economy.

Tourism Satellite Account (TSA) is a set of data tables based around analyses of data on both expenditure by tourists, and on business sectors which serve tourists.

A TSA provides a much enhanced set of statistics which are more accurate than by taking the results of individual surveys alone. These data include the contribution of tourism to the economy, and the number of jobs supported by tourism, for example. A TSA also opens up possibilities for modelling and analysis.

The TSA allows for the harmonization and reconciliation of tourism statistics from an economic (National Accounts) perspective. This enables the generation of tourism economic data (such as Tourism Direct GDP) that is comparable with other economic statistics.

The TSA can be seen as a set of 10 summary tables, each with their underlying data:

♦ inbound, domestic tourism and outbound tourism expenditure,

♦ internal tourism expenditure,

♦ production accounts of tourism industries,

♦ the Gross Value Added (GVA) and Gross Domestic Product (GDP) attributable to tourism,

♦ employment,

♦ investment,

♦ government consumption, and

♦ non-monetary indicators.

ॐ

IV
Travel Formalities

Introduction

A travel document is an identity document issued by a government or international treaty organization to facilitate the movement of individuals or small groups of persons across international boundaries following international agreements. The need of travel documents arise as they usually assure other governments that the bearer may return to the issuing country, and are often issued in booklet form to allow other governments to place visas as well as entry and exit stamps into them. The most common travel document is a passport, which usually gives the bearer more privileges like visa-free access to certain countries.

Travel Documents

The Travel documents which are required while travelling for international and domestic travel are few but important .A person cannot travel without possessing them especially in case of international travel .Passengers are required to ensure that they are in possession of all documents necessary for travel, apart from their tickets.

For domestic travel within India, valid photo identification, namely ·Valid Passport ·PAN card issued by the Income Tax department ·Election Photo Identification Card ·Valid Driving License ·Photo identity card issued by the employer, being government and reputed private sector organizations ·Photo Credit Card ·Children should carry their school identification cards or any other photo identification proof, ·Valid birth certificates of infants ·

A passport is a document, issued by a national government, which certifies the identity and nationality of its holder for the purpose of international travel. There are different elements of identity in passport .They are name, date of birth, sex, and place of birth. It is an official document issued by a competent public authority or official; usually the sovereign head of the country. Throughout world there are different issuing authorities in different countries.Passport is a privilege issued to citizens of a country, or aliens residing in that country, for a period of time. It is every citizen's birthright.The rights to consular protection arise from international agreements, and the right to return arises from the laws of the issuing country.

VISA "Visitors Intended to stay abroad

Visa is a document showing that a person is authorized to enter the territory for which it was issued subject to permission of an immigration official at the time of the actual entry. As per TIM, a Visa is an entry in a passport or other travel document made by a consular official of a government to indicate that the bearer has been granted authority to enter or re-enter the country concerned.

Types of Travel Documents

There are different types of travel documents like Passport and VISA.

Passport are of different types:

1) Tourist Passport/ Regular Passport–It is the most common form of passport, issued to citizens and other nationals. Occasionally, children are registered within the parents' passport, making it equivalent to a family passport

2) Official Passport/ Service Passport –It is issued to government employees for work-related travel, and their accompanying dependants.

3) Diplomatic passport – It is issued to diplomats of a country and their accompanying dependents for official international travel and residence.

4) Emergency Passport (also called temporary passport) –Emergency passport is issued to persons whose passports were lost or stolen, without time to obtain a replacement.

Other types of Passport include: 1) British Emergency Passport-It is a collective passport which is issued to defined groups for travel together to particular destinations, such as a group of school children on a school trip. Family passport –It is issued to an entire family. There is one passport holder, who may travel alone or with other family members included in the passport. A family member who is not the passport holder cannot use the passport for travel without the passport holder. Few countries now issue family passports; for example, all the EU countries and Canada require each child to have his or her own passport.

Other type of travel documents

Laissez-passer— It is issued by national governments or international organizations such as the U.N.as emergency passports, travel on humanitarian grounds, or for official travel.

Interpol Travel Document— Issued by Interpol to police officers for official travel, allowing them to bypass certain visa restrictions in certain member states when investigating transnational crime.

Certificate of identity (also called alien's passport, or informally, a Travel Document) — Issued under certain circumstances, such as statelessness, to non-citizen residents. An example is the "Nansen passport" .Sometimes issued as an internal passport to non-residents.

Refugee travel document — Issued to a refugee by the state in which she or he currently resides allowing them to travel outside that state and to return. It is made necessary because refugees are unlikely to be able to obtain passports from their state of nationality.

Permits-Many types of travel permit exist around the world. Some, like the U.S. Re-entry Permit, and Japan Re-entry Permit, allow residents of those countries who are unable to obtain a permit to travel outside the country and return.

Chinese Travel Document - Issued by the People's Republic of China to Chinese citizens in lieu of a passport.

Hajj passport— a special passport used only for Hajjand Umbra pilgrimage to Mecca and Medina.

VISA

A few of the commonly utilized visa categories are outlined below.

1) Temporary VISA-The following VISA come under temporary VISA.

A) Tourist/Visitor Visas- Available to all visitors coming to any country for business or pleasure.

B) Treaty and Investor Visas- Investors and traders and their employees may receive visas to carry on their businesses.

C) Student Visas- Persons seeking to pursue a full course of study at a school are eligible for a visa for the course of their study plus, in some cases, a period for practical training in their field of study.

D) H-1B Specialty Occupation (Professionals) Visas- Professional workers with at least a bachelor's degree (or its equivalent work experience) may be eligible for a non-immigrant visa if their employers can demonstrate that they are to be paid at least the prevailing wage for the position.

E) J-1 and Q-1 Exchange Visitor Visas- Persons coming to the country for approved exchange program may be eligible for the J-1 Exchange Visitor's visa. J-1 programs often cover students, short-term scholars, business trainees, teachers, professors and research scholars, specialists, international visitors, government visitors, etc

Other types include: Project Visa ,Gratis Visa ,Journalist Visa , Business Visa , Missionary Visa , Mountaineering Visa ,Medical & Medical Attendant Visa I , Universal Visa , Diplomatic/Official/UN Official Visa , Transit Visa ,Entry Visa ,Tourist Visa ,Employment Visa , Research Visa

5. Health Regulations

The health regulations form an integral part of travel documentation process. No travel documentation process can be complete without following health regulations. Any person, Foreigner or Indian, (excluding infants below six months) arriving by air or sea without a vaccination certificate of yellow fever shall be kept in quarantine isolation for a period up to six days. Some countries require visitors to take some precautionary vaccinations prior to a visit. These are normally for Yellow Fever & Cholera infected zones. Pax must have these vaccinations endorsed in a booklet, format for which is prescribed by the WHO. The following types of persons are exempted from production yellow fever vaccination certificate: Infants below the age of six months are exempted. , Any person suffering from some chronic illness and poor resistance is thereby exempted from being vaccination

6. Currency Regulations

Currency regulations are imposed to check the inflow and outflow of currency from one country to another. There is a limit of currency which an individual as tourist can carry from origin to destination. Currency Regulations are currency regulations for each country. This includes details of Currency Import & Export from one place to another .Import of currency includes how much of currency can a passenger bring into the country. Export of currency include how much Foreign Exchange can a passenger carry out of the country. Foreign currencies include currency notes, traveller's cheques, cheques, drafts etc. (Re) exchange only through banks and authorized money exchange points.

7.Customs Regulations includes information on Customs regulations for all countries.

This information is about what a passenger can bring into and take out of a country without having to pay duty. It is also known as the Duty-free allowance of a passenger. Free import (import by non-residents, however, is only permitted if they enter India for a stay of not less than 24 hours and not more than 6 months, provided they visit India not more than once a month)

7. Travel Insurance

Travel insurance is the insurance that is intended to cover medical expenses ,trip cancellations, lost luggage ,flight accidents, and other expenses incurred while travelling either internationally or one's own country. Travel Insurance is always advisable to carry Insurance while travelling abroad. It is also mandatory for many countries. It covers several risks associated with travel. It should be pre-purchased and must remain valid for the duration of trip. It is useful in covering several risks, such as Loss of Advance, Deposit, Travel Delays, Medical & Related Expenses Interruption / Curtailment, Returning to Resume, Travel Personal, Accident Luggage, and Personal Effects & Money Loss Personal Liability.

The concept of travel documentation has grown over the past few decades and now relative inclusions have been made in its records. Travel documents are necessary to make travel safe and sound. It is helping in smooth international travels and within a region, area. Travel documents are the need of the hour and the very basic and initial steps to be a tool for successful travels. Based on this, the number of international arrivals and departures is booming high every year. Travel documents make travel process valid, authentic and regulates many illegal activities. Documentation is required in order to have control on all the unethical practices in travel and trade business. Visa , passport have long proved to the best Identification cards . The travel journey cannot be completed without the travel documents which in turn help in uniting the world by "one process one world"

Factors influencing growth of Tourism

a.Demographic Factors

The composition of the population in a country plays a major role in affecting many dynamic industries like the tourism industry. These factors primarily include age, income level and family members earning, size of the household, nationality, gender, culture, food habits, climate, etc. The income of the family members determines the nature of travel, place of travel, amount spent on travelling and on the destination amenities, time spent in the destination, loyalty to the travel brands and agencies and sources and amount of gathering information. On the other hand, low income travellers or budget travellers or back packers do not consider it important to gather information before travelling and they prefer travelling to lesser known destinations with minimum amenities and low cost facilities.

Another demographic factor that affects the tourism in a destination is the age of the visitors. For Example the youngsters would enjoy the adventure activities like rafting, bungee jumping, paragliding and similar activities in a destination where the same destination could be leisure or spiritual destination for the elder or old age visitors.

Gender is another important demographic factor which influences the growth of tourism in a place. Arrivals of more number of female visitors in place would demand more shopping outlets like souvenir shops which would change the shopping trends in the destination, whereas the male visitors would demand for an altogether different market drifts.

Nativity is an important factor that determines choices and preferences for accommodation, transportation and recreational activities. For instance, Europeans are more interested in culture and tradition of a place whereas the British tourists would indulge themselves more into fun and leisure activities.

The household size of the visitors can highly influence the growth of tourism in a destination as the group with children would have more inclination for all the activities in the destination as the children are inquisitive in nature and curious for new things where as the a mature couple in a destination would only limit themselves to certain amount of things which are comfortable to get and which they are interested in.

Technological Factors

Technological changes in tourism involve several factors like changing business intervention, better communication, modern mass media techniques, new practices in transportation and improvement in basic facilities like water supply and easier accessibility to all types of visitors. A massive effect on growth tourism is brought from the rapid increase in online booking trends. This technological support has provided a lot of opportunity to the consumers to avail all the services online which were earlier only feasible after reaching at the destination. Since the visitors have become aware of the online booking facilities and the suppliers have acquired a platform to sell their products online, it has become one of the biggest factors in affecting the growth of tourism business.Holiday bookings and airlines and railways booking have dramatically increased after the boost in the online market. Along with transportation facilities, the accommodation services have also found a place in the online market and are increasing with time. All type of hotels, home stays, home exchange programs and bed and breakfast services all over the world are connected to each other and also to the consumers through various social media sites. The increase in the usage of the social media sites has also generated interest in the visitors. The social media and travel blogs play a prime role in promoting the destinations and providing a virtual tour to the potential travelers. The technological advancement has also helped many destinations to get connected with the rest of world through cruises, railways, roads and aviation.

Economic Factors

Travelling to any destination far or near require some amount of disposable income from the travelers. Whether it is a luxurious Psychocentric destination or an allocentric destination, it would consume some amount of income from the tourists for the conveyance, food and lodging and performing several other activities. The tourists with high disposable income would spend more in any destination than the tourists having less disposable income. The economic factor thus plays an important role in making or breaking of the tourism industry.

Environmental Factors

Good climate has always been a major factor to attract tourists from different parts of the world. Pleasant breeze, warm sunshine, cool weather has always attracted tourists towards it. The people who hail from the planes or the hot climatic regions always prefer to travel towards the hills stations and the places which are prone to snow fall. The travellers from the western countries are attracted towards the countries near the equatorial region to experience the sun, sand and sea phenomena. Sun rising from the valleys, beautiful scenic beauty, green meadows, and waterfalls, sunset at the beach, snow fall in the mountains, fresh water lakes and even rains in the tropics are a matter of motivation for different types of tourists coming from different climatic regions of the world.

Socio-Cultural Factors

Culture of a place with its unique features has been a matter of attraction for the tourists since ages. Different civilizations emerged from different parts of the world have very distinctive features amongst themselves to portray their traditions and the people of the places. When tourists from a different cultural background travel towards a new culture, he/she also takes own culture along with them through which cultural exchange and cultural hybridization take place. The socio-cultural standards of any region would include the traditional attires, ornaments, food habits, lifestyle, folk songs and dances and the way of life, which largely defines a particular tribe or race.

Historical and Religious Factors

Every place has its different historical perspectives which have the proof of it through its ancient forts, palaces, monuments and memorials. Many tourists are attracted to the legacy of the rich historical heritage of a place. Religious or pilgrimage tourism is one of those forms of tourism which attracts large number of tourists. The religious shrines or different cultures attract the visitors for the attainment of inner peace and sanctity. People travel to get blessings of their favorite deities. Religious reasons force people to travel at all the occasions may it be birth, adolescence, marriage or death, people travel to their respective gods and goddesses to satisfy their soul and bring peace to their mind, body and family members.

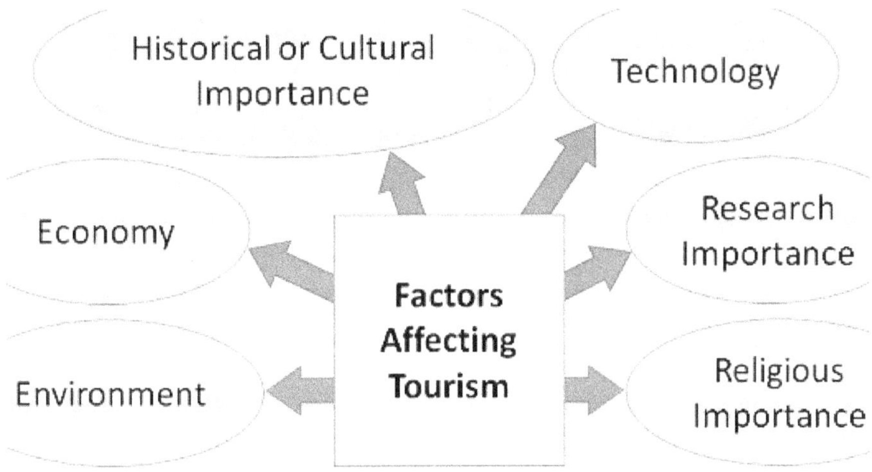

Enter Caption

Multidisciplinary Approach

To learn the elements of tourism, it becomes necessary to study all the different areas which are related to tourism. The different approaches to study tourism include: ü Institutional Approach ü Product Approach ü

Managerial Approach ü Economic Approach ü Cost-Benefit Approach ü Sociological Approach ü Geographical Approach ü Environmental Approach ü Historical Approach ü Interdisciplinary Approach

Institutional Approach

The institutional approach to study tourism is one of the major approaches which take into account the institutions as the name depicts and the intermediaries which work towards providing tourism services to the customers. These include the tour operators who are basically the wholesalers of travel packages and the travel agents who act as intermediaries between the tour operators and the potential travellers. Apart from them, there are transportation services provided by the airlines companies, car rental companies, railways and cruises who sell their tickets in bulk to the tour operators and travel agencies and also directly to the consumers which are an important institutional link between the service providers and the customers.

Product Approach

The product approach is to study tourism involves all the activities related to tourism products ranging from manufacturing of the products, marketing to consumption of them by the consumers. It would involve understanding the creation or production of different tourism products like the airline seats and hotels rooms. Once they are available to the customers the next step is to market or promote them through different promotional modes like the print media which includes newspapers, magazines, brochures, electronic media like advertisements in the television, promotional messages in mobile phones with attractive offers like discounts can really help promote these services and products to the potential customers.

Managerial Approach

This approach is enterprise or firm oriented approach that emphasizes mainly on management activities which are required to manage perform tourism practices. It is a micro economic in nature that may include management activities like organizing, planning, controlling, research and development, costing, marketing and promotions. Management functions are a must in every field which needs to be working in a planned and organized manner. Tourism is one such business which if preceded in an unplanned way or not manage properly can damage not only the environment of the destination but also the community serving the customers would affect adversely. Hence, management approaches are a vital force to perform the tourism related activities and keep a check on the positive and negative analysis of the activities taking place in the destination.

Economic Approach

This approach relates tourism towards economic development of the place and people where tourism is practiced. The economic approach focuses upon the economic benefits caused by practicing tourism like empowerment of the community, revenue generated out of the tourism activities, employment opportunities provided to the locals and foreign exchange gained by the tourism products and foreign travelers. Thus, the economic approach in tourism helps the students to understand the economic implications of the tourism on the economy. This is related to the effects which implies by tourism on countries economy and tourism development on the basis of economic aspects

The important economic effects are:

a) Foreign Currency Effect: Tourism is one of the important sources for earning foreign currency. But from the point of view of seeing its effect on the economy it becomes necessary to see what the net foreign currency receipt is. So, the imports of investment and consumer goods required by tourists have to be deducted from the country's gross receipts from foreign tourism.

b) Income Effect: Income Effect refers to the direct income earned that resulting from the expenditure made by the tourists. It is also the indirect income which results from the multiplier effect i.e., when the first recipient spends a part of his income again. For example: an accommodation owner spends part of his earnings on buying grocery for his self-consumption; here income earned by one is generating income for some other also.

c) Employment Effect: Tourism is a labor intensive industry which creates both direct and indirect employment like jobs in the airline industry or the hotels. These are examples of direct employment and the suppliers of food beverages are the sources of indirect employment. Studies show that the employment effect is much higher in the developing countries than developed countries.

V

Impacts of Tourism

Tourism Impacts

The main positive economic impacts of tourism relate to foreign exchange earnings, contributions to government revenues, generation of employment and business opportunities. Tourism expenditures, the export and import of related goods and services generate income to the host economy.Tourism is a labor intensive industry and operates 24 hours a day, seven days a week. There are many opportunities for employment for young people and for people interested in part time or casual work. While some of the employment is skilled, there are also opportunities for people less skilled and who lack formal qualifications. Direct economic benefits are those economic benefits that are very obvious and directly connected with tourism field such as hotels, transportations, employment etc. Indirect and induced effects are sometimes collectively called secondary effects. The total economic impact of tourism is the sum of direct, indirect, and induced effects within a region.

Direct effects are production changes associated with the immediate effects of changes in tourism expenditures. For example, an increase in the number of tourists staying overnight in hotels would directly yield increased sales in the hotel sector. The additional hotel sales and associated changes in hotel payments for wages and salaries, taxes, and supplies and services are direct effects of the tourist spending. Indirect effects are the production changes resulting from various rounds of re-spending of the hotel industry's receipts in other backward-linked industries (i.e., industries supplying products and services to hotels). Changes in sales, jobs, and income in the linen supply industry, for example, represent indirect effects of changes in hotel sales. Businesses supplying products and services to the linen supply industry represent another round of indirect effects, eventually linking hotels to varying degrees to many other economic sectors in the region. Induced effects are the changes in economic activity resulting from household spending of income earned directly or indirectly as a result of tourism spending.

Direct Impact of Tourism

The direct impact of tourism is noticed mainly in the primary sectors such as hotels and lodging, restaurants, transport, entertainment and retail. Direct impact refers to the changes occurring in sales, job generation, tax revenues and income accruals due to changes in tourism expenditure patterns. More number of tourists staying in hotels will increase sales and revenue accruals in the hotel sector. These increased sales and related changes in wage / salary payments, tax revenues, demands for goods and services are the direct impacts of more tourists spending. It may be inferred that the direct impact of tourism is to induce income and employment, converting a large percentage of sales into direct income and employment.

Indirect Impact of Tourism

The indirect impact of tourism refers to the changes that result due to re-spending of the primary tourism sectors in backward linked sectors. Through its indirect impact, tourism has the potential to impact almost every sector of the economy. . In this way, the primary sectors of the tourism industry are linked indirectly through different degrees to other economic sectors in the area.

Induced Impact of Tourism Induced impact of tourism refers to changes in economic activity primarily reflected in changes in household spending of income earned either directly or indirectly from tourism. The workers in hotels, restaurants, retail shops and their associated suppliers and partners are paid wages out of spending incurred directly or indirectly through tourism. These employees in turn spend their wages on housing, food, transport and other goods and services required for their daily needs.

a.*Economic Impacts of Tourism*

There are other economic impacts of tourism that do not fall under the direct, indirect and induced categories.

Impact on Prices: Tourist activity, especially during the 'tourism season' can artificially inflate prices of hotel rooms, restaurants and retail shops in the area

Impact on Quality / Quantity of Goods / Services: Tourism can trigger a wider variety of goods and services to become available in an area. The quality of these goods and services can be higher or lower than without tourist activity.

Impact on Property Taxes / Other Taxes: More tourist activity can lead to higher levels of taxation with businesses being taxed more heavily for the tourist infrastructure and services that will have to be put in place such as roads, bridges, provisioning for electricity and water.

Social and Environmental Impacts: Tourism can have both positive and negative social and environmental impacts in the area. For example, more tourists will result in more traffic and this can result in more air pollution. Improved amenities can result in more elderly person or a variety of businesses to relocate to an area changing its social demography and characteristics.

b.*Social Impacts of Tourism.*

i) *Positive Impacts.*

a. All Inclusive Characteristics.

Tourism is no more the privilege of a chosen few who prefers just the luxurious components of the industry. The tourist market globally configures very diverse segments encompassing geographical background, demographics categories, and the like. Social tourism is yet another form of tourism that brings people with limited means to the mainstream pradding them to visit and enjoy tourism destinations. "Social tourism is a type of tourism practiced by lowincome groups, and which is rendered possible and facilitated by entirely separate and therefore easily recognisable services. This form of tourism helps people with limited budget travel with assistance from NGO's incentives and schemes under budget travel extended by the public system of tourism, and discounts offered by the private sector agencies.

b. Social Stability and Peace.

Diplomacy. This diplomacy constitutes cultural relations not at the government level, but at the level of the common citizens of countries. Tourism fosters social stability by instilling noble ideas and free thoughts thorough healthy interactions and various other transactions between the hosts and the guests wherein both are benefited. It broadens the mind of people and as a result, there is increased acceptance, mutual trust, and more tolerance. These factors contribute profusely towards strengthening social stability and world peace.

c. Appreciation of Social Norms, Values, and Practices

Sociologists categorically print out that as tourists visit several nations and regions and get back to their respective countries their vibes in appreciating own countries and regions become very profound. It is indicated that tourists tend to see their countries in a newer light and value tremendously the intricate aspects of their social customs and practices. Another dimension here is that when tourists see better practices in the areas they visit, there is dire enthusiasm built up in them.

d. The Educative Value and Social Upliftment.

Tourism is in a way education without classrooms. The interpersonal learning developed during interactions between the tourists and the host community is certainly an enriching experience for both the parties. The new vision acquired as a result of different engagements with tourism - as tourist, local community, employer or employee will definitely have positive reflections on the society as well.

e. Contribution to Social Capital.

Tourism ushers social progress in manifold ways. In addition to the advancements made in the sphere of infrastructure and superstructure, destinations experience immense growth as regards educational institutions, health centres, pollution control systems, intensive security, cultural institutions, etc. Social welfare measures receive excellent impetus as a result of tourism making a mark in the destination. Enhanced livelihood sustenance programmes have gained grounds in many a tourist centre as an offshoot of such measures. Artisans are trained to improve the quality of their works. Social enterprises including rehabilitation centres, de-addiction centres, product innovation & development institutions, and local empowerment agencies are having a productive time due to the regular influx of tourists and the genuine interest taken by voluntary tourists and other stakeholders

ii) *Negative Impacts.*

a. Degeneration of Tourism Centres. Tourism is an avenue misused and exploited by antisocial elements. It is the responsibility of the local communities to properly guide the tourists in such a way so as to avoid dangerous places and areas. Owing to the prostitution, child abuse, drug trafficking, robbery and sexual assault on tourists, the image of many destinations have been eroded.

b. Resentment and Hospitality of the Host Population.

Resentment of tourists by the host population as described by Doxey's Irridex (Irritation Index) is found in some destinations. There are several reasons attributed to the host quest conflicts. One main reason is the sharing of local facilities and resources. When tourists start using the same resources which the host population feels that are meant for them the spurt in conflict arise.

c. Demonstration Effect.

When certain members of the host community get enchanted by the lifestyle of the tourists and start imitating them ,the local culture and values suffer. There is some kind of erosion of values as the host community members, particularly the youngsters discard their social standing and etiquettes and start following the tourists' activities. The foundation of the society itself is shaken. Now a day's hosts start following the dressing pattern and fashion of tourists in many destinations.

d. Human Rights Abuse.

Exploitation of the local community by tourists is increasing day by day. As criminals and other miscreants enter, the tourism destinations in the garb of tourists, the crimes committed goes overboard. They start exploiting the host community by cheaper means. Sexual abuse, narcoticism, smuggling, poaching, etc., are rampant in many wildlife tourism destinations and hill stations.

Another side of the problem is the displacement of the local population when their lands are taken over for the tourism development.

Antagonism of Hosts. When there is unwanted noise, congestion, drunkenness, voyeurism, gambling, rowdiness and other excesses occurring in tourism centres, it results in antagonism by the hosts.

Cultural Relations and International Co-Operation.

Tourism plays a signature role in promoting cultural relations and forging international co-operation. Cultural organisations across the world are making their presence felt owing to the impetus provided by tourism. In the present day, tourism is instrumental in the inception of several cultural institutions. Plenty of cultural exchange programmes are being organised at the global level. This point out that tourism is intertwined with the cultural relations policies of many nations.

. Promotion of Cultural Values.

When tourism supports cultural values, attitude, and behaviour of the host communities in various destinations, one can observe that there is finest hospitality and service excellence. The host communities take pride in their cultural traditions. Tourism serves as a driving force to restore cultural vibrancy and attributes of the local population.

. Economic Value of Cultural Sites.

Any cultural auditing will unveil the economic advantages of protecting and maintaining a cultural site. For example, there are lots of caves which are astounding tourism attractions. If it would have been left uncared for destruction, the revenue sources are being blocked. Similar is the case with most of the cultural manifestations.

Cultural Tourism and Income Generation.

Tourism contributes to the welfare of the local community in manifold ways. When fairs and festivals are rejuvenated to amuse the tourists, the host population is able to be performers or spectators of the events. The cultural programmes and revived monuments increase the inflow of tourists due to which plenty of business opportunities shall arise in the tourist places. This will improve their job and earning prospects. The host community can earn a good income. Selling antiques and souvenir articles to tourists is another source of income.

Negative Cultural Impacts:

a. Commoditisation of Culture.

Cultural artifacts and events attract the tourists and they take great interest in enjoying them. Sometimes, the destination promoters are neglecting the richness of the cultural masterpieces and treating them as mere products or resources to invigorate the tourists. This happens even with deep-rooted traditional art forms. For the sake of formulating the art forms and artefacts as products to amuse the tourists, a lot of compromises are taking place.

b. Loss of Authenticity.

This is another related negative impact. In the name of entertainment of tourists, there are tampering and mutilations happening with respect to indigenous cultural expressions of profound importance. In the process, the authenticity is being lost. Fake products are crafted and packages as genuine cultural artefacts. The tourists in a way are cheated and such tendencies from the destination promotes can eventually rebound wherein through negative word of mouth publicity the destination image will suffer. Staged authenticity or stage-managing the art forms for tourist's enjoyment does not necessarily bring the desired results.

c.Disrespect of Local Customs.

Tourists are expected to respect local customs, codes, manners, and observances. When they violate the beliefs and values due to attitudinal problems or sheer carelessness, it leads to conflicts. The irresponsible conduct of tourists at the destination by engaging in littering, drug trafficking, irritable behaviour, hooliganism, animosity towards hosts, etc. can hamper the relationship between the hosts and the guests.

d. Museumisation of Culture.

As part of ethnic tourism, which promotes intimate contact the indigenous community, nowadays special tours are being arranged to their habitats. This is a tight ropewalk as the tours can be construed as an intrusion into the privacy of the native habitats.

e. Fashion and Obscene Conduct. Tourism centres will have many traditional concepts as regards the dress codes for the people both visitors and the locals. In the name of fashion and modernity, tourists are sometimes found to overlook the etiquettes followed in the destination. Their fashion could be obscene conduct for the host community.

f. Food Observances. Tourists cannot always expect the food items they have in their own native or other centres at the destination.

g. Child Labour and Child Sex Tourism. This is a cultural hazard due to fast-paced tourism growth. Children doing jobs in restaurant, hotels, wayside amenities, and other outlets. Sexual exploitation of children who perform art forms for entertaining the tourists is also on the rise

Socio-Cultural Considerations in Tourism Planning.

The planners must necessarily take into account the following socio-cultural perspectives while planning tourism ventures.

a. Standardisation of Tourism Projects.

b. Planned and Controlled Tourism Development.

c. Preservation of Cultural Sites.

d. Diversification of Tourism Products for Budget and Accessible tourism

f. Tourism Amenities.

g. Marketing Support of Souvenir Articles.

h. Integration of Policy and Planning.

c.*Environmental Impact of Tourism*

Pristine natural resources and environment have always been the critical requirements of successful tourism. Tourists look for attractive natural sources, tourism activities and the like. The relationship between tourism and environment has crossed four stages over the years since its inception

Negative Impacts

Direct Impact: It has direct effects on the environment of the destination.

a) Tourist Movements: When a tourist wades out in beach, large portions of the coral and fish life around the boat jetties are killed. Souvenir trade like shells, shell jewelry etc is done by the removal of life forms. This could be seen in Lakshadweep where trampling of shallow water corals is common.

b) Dumping of Solid Waste: Littering of plastic, cans, bottles, poly-ethylene, eatables, leaflets, coconut wastes etc are a common sight in many islands and beaches. Added to it, dumping of human waste and defection is a major problem in many beaches. Oil spillage by motor boats and ships while transporting tourists is another problem. In mountain areas, trekking tourists generate a great deal of waste. They leave behind garbage, oxygen cylinders and even camping materials.

c) Deforestation: It has been a trend to clear forests in order to develop resorts, hotels, fishing farms, lying lines of transport and the like in order to cater to tourist interests. This has created havoc in the ecosystem.

d) Water Pollution: It has been found that there is a drastic decline of coral reefs due to the sewage water directly being released into rivers, oceans and the like. Construction of buildings along the coastline has altered the patterns of sand movement. Global warming caused by tourism activity leads to rising in sea temperatures. It is also found that there is increased pressure in sewage treatment plants that overflows due to heavy tourist activity. In addition, discharge of sewage into water bodies due to recreational boating and cruises have lead to the destruction of shell-fish locations. Dal Lake in Srinagar is heavily polluted and weeded due to the release of an incredible amount of fecal matter and pathogenic materials from house boats.

e) Mountains: They account for 15-20% of world tourism. Some of the environmental problems include trail degradation, deposition of rubbish along the trails, deforestation due to excessive firewood use and traffic emissions of nitrogen oxides, hydrocarbons and lead.

f) Wildlife: This accounts for 10% of the international tourism. The main impacts of tourism are disruption in the feeding and breeding pattern of animals. It also alters their eating habits. Feeding patterns of wildlife is indirectly affected by littering as they eat the waste. Some of the factors that contribute to the wildlife variations include difference in breeding seasons and behaviors, lifecycle, maturity, alarm behaviors and ecological niche competition. Wildlife can be adversely affected by the construction and maintenance of tourist infrastructure and by tourist activities.

g) Climate Change: Climate scientists have generally agreed that earth temperature has increased due to the green house gases. CO2 is generated with the fossil fuels such as coal, oil and natural gas or due to changes in landscape, through deforestation. In the long-run, accumulation of CO in the atmosphere can cause global climate change. Air travel such as passenger jets is also a major contributor to the green house effects.

h) Air Pollution: Most of the tourism related air pollution come from automobiles. Due to the increase in transportation, number of tourists has been increasing thus causing increased air pollution. One consequence of this is increase in air transport. Tourism accounts for more than 60% of air travel and is responsible for an important share of air emissions. Added to it automobiles emit carbon monoxide.

i) Noise Pollution: Noise pollution from airlines, cars and buses as well as recreational vehicles such as snowmobiles and jet skis is a problem of modern life. It increases stress and even hearing loss for humans, it causes distress to wildlife especially in sensitive areas.

j) Aesthetic and Cultural Impacts: Tourism can reduce the aesthetic appearance of destination due to high rise buildings, creating visual pollution. For example, due to high rise hotels in Jerusalem, it has damaged cities with architectural beauty.

k) Impact on Local communities: Due to tourism activities, the character of the local people may get altered. The cultural and aesthetic aspects of these communities may be shattered due to the development of tourist activity.

l) Depletion of Ozone Layer: The ozone layer that absorbs harmful ultra violet(UV) rays is located at an altitude 12-50 kms in the upper atmosphere, thus protecting earth. The tourism industry could cause direct impact, due to the construction of new developments for tourists. Refrigerators, air-conditioners and propellers in aerosol spray cars, amongst others are widely used by hotel and tourism industry, which may cause depletion in ozone layer.

Physical Impacts of Tourism Development

Construction Activities and Infrastructure Development: The development of tourism facilities such as accommodation, water supplies, restaurants and recreation facilities can lead to sand mining in beaches causing sand erosion. Road and airport construction can lead to land degradation and loss of wildlife habits and deterioration of scenery.

Deforestation and Intensified or Unsustainable Use of Land: In order to construct ski-resorts, accommodation and the like, constantly forests are cleared. Even coastal wetlands are often drained and filled when there is a lack of suitable sites for construction of tourism facilities and infrastructure.

Marine Development: Over building and expensive paving of shorelines can result in the destruction of habitats and disruption of land-sea connection (such as seaturtle nesting spots). Shoreline development, increased sediments in the water, trampling by tourists and divers, ship groundings, pollution from sewage, over fishing and fishing with poisons and explosives destroy the coral island.

Hazard Introduction Effect: Introduction of hazardous weeds, predators and diseases could affect the natural environment. Tourists may also introduce hazards from negative behaviors such as fuel leakage or disposal, soap chemicals from washing, littering and the like.

Infrastructural Development: Building up of resorts, hotels, laying down of transport and communication, setting up of golf courses, eating joints and the like in a destination does hamper the ecosystem.

Hiking, Snorkeling and Diving: Snorkeling and diving cause damage to corals under the sea, which is a source of existence for under water species.

Tourist Activities within National Parks: Due to heavy visitor and traffic congestion, many tourist destinations have been greatly impacted by this problem. It could also affect and vandalize sites of cultural significance. Damage to cultural resources is more dangerous and with passage of time, it could affect the natural resources.

Recreational Boating: The most significant problem with this activity is dumping of sewage into water bodies thus flushing shell fish beds. Sewage is directly dumped into sea by several cruises, which contains pathogens thus adversely affecting human health and endanger species inside water. Diseases could be potentially transmitted through contact with human feacal discharge and / or ingestion thus contaminating shell fish, causing an increase in diseases like typhoid fever, dysentery, infections hepatitis etc.

Water and Adventure Sports: Scuba diving, deep sea diving, snorkeling etc if done on a massive scale will affect marine ecosystems. Marine life is also disturbed by high speed cruising tourist boats. For example, snorkeling is taking toll on the corals of Lakshadweep.

Positive Impacts

Despite its many adverse impacts, tourism can have positive impacts on both natural and artificially constructed environments as well as on destination communities. Tourism has motivated the preservation of sensitive ecosystems. It focuses on cultural and historic sites that could be the impetus for the preservation and rehabilitation of existing historic sites, buildings and monuments. In addition, the economic benefits of tourism partially balance the negative environmental impacts. Local communities in and around the national parks are benefited by the income that they get from tourism. The parks attract more visitors to these communities, resulting in increased employment opportunities and an improved standard of living.

Upstream and Downstream Impacts Hotels can exert "upstream" influence on its suppliers to provide products that minimize environmental impacts through supplier relations. Similarly travel services such as tour operators can have "downstream" impacts by influencing tourists through education and provision of option to reduce resource use. For example, hotels can give guests the option not to have their linens washed daily and cruise lines can limit the number of tourists that go ashore to a sensitive destination. Downstream influence through tourism education could be an attempt towards reducing the impact on environment. In addition, tour operators specializing in ecotourism can influence their customers through the provision of environmental guidelines before and during trips.

The Concept of Tourism Multiplier

Tourism being a multi-faceted and interdisciplinary industry has a great potential in generating income and employment (direct and indirect). Tourism, being one of the largest industries for many countries, has a high multiplier effect. The inflow of money from Tourist Generating Region to Tourist Destination Region through various sectors of the economy is very high which contributes to the economic development. Tourism is on higher trajectory of creation as it not only creates jobs in its own tertiary sector, it also reassures growth in the related primary and secondary sectors of industry. This phenomenon is known as the multiplier effect. In other words, how many times a money spent by a tourist circulates in a particular country's economy. Money spent in a hotel or restaurant helps to create jobs directly in the hotel premises. It also generates jobs indirectly in related or allied industry elsewhere in the economy. For example, the hotel buys food from local farmers or market supplier, who may spend some amount of this money on clothes or other products. Tourists often buy souvenirs from destination this increases demand for local products, which upsurges secondary employment in locally. The multiplier effects continue or have ripple effect until the money in due course 'leaks' from the economy through imports or other methods.

Multiplier concept is based on Keynesian analysis. It tracks the money spent by the tourists as it filters through the economy. The revenue decreases in a geometric progression at each round as a result of leakages.

Tourism Expenditure and Multiplier Tourism Expenditure can be broadly divided into three types. Namely · Direct Expenditure, · Indirect Expenditure, and · Induced Expenditure

Direct Tourism Expenditure consists of expenditures by the tourists on goods and services on hotels, shops, and other tourism related services. It is otherwise known as the tourist's initial spending which creates direct revenue.

Indirect Tourism Expenditure includes the transaction between businesses caused by direct tourism expenditures. It is otherwise known as the initial process of re-spending i.e., employees' salary. For example, purchase made by hotels from local suppliers and goods bought by suppliers from the wholesalers.

Induced Tourism Expenditure consists of increase consumption resulting from increase in income provided by direct tourism expenditure. It is otherwise known as the secondary process For example, the employees of the hotel purchase goods and services otherwise known as re-spending.

Types of Multiplier

According to Lickorish and Jenkins, tourist multipliers can be classified into five main broad categories:

1. Sales or transaction multiplier: The sales or transaction multiplier measures direct, indirect and induced turnover generated by extra unit of tourism expenditures or additional business turnover.

2. Output or production multiplier: The output or production multiplier measures the extra production and accounts an increase in stock levels at hotels, restaurants and shops as a result of increase in commercial or trading activities. The output multipliers are mainly concerned with actual levels or changes in production or output rather than the volume of sales or value.

3. Income multiplier: An income multiplier measures the income (receipt) generated by an additional unit of tourist expenditure. The salaries remunerated to overseas residents are not counted, only the proportion of

these that has been spent in the area should be included while measuring Income multiplier.

4. Employment multipliers: Employment multipliers measure the effects of extra economic activities on employment i.e., the increased number of primary and secondary jobs generated by an extra unit of tourism expenditure. This multiplier can be expressed in namely direct and indirect employment.

5. The official or government revenue tourism multiplier: It indicates the net value ie, taxes less subsidies, of government income from tourism.

Use of Multiplier

Multiplier is a tool used to analyze the economic effect of increase in tourism expenditure and its influence on other sectors of the economy. The value of multiplier depends on the particular features of the tourism in the area studied and the characteristics of the local economy.

Global Efforts to Mitigate Environmental Impacts of Tourism

Several efforts in various directions have been taken by organizations globally to mitigate environmental impacts of tourism.

Government Efforts:

It was as early as 1940s that the World Union of Conservation of Natural Resources were constituted to conserve nature and natural resources in order to promote active conservation and planned use of location with indispensable features.

It encompassed the need for 1) integration of environmental protection in physical planning policies, 2) dealing with the issue of tourist capital protection at the global level, 3) uniformity in national environmental practices and 4) setting up of an inventory of tourism resources friendly.

Financial Contributions: Tourism can contribute directly to conserve sensitive areas and habitat. Revenue from park entrance fees and similar sources could be used for the protection and management of environmentally sensitive areas. Special fees for park operations or conservation activities can be allocated for tourists or tour-operators. User fees, income taxes, taxes on sales or rental of recreation equipment and license fees for activities such as hunting and fishing can provide governments with the funds needed to manage natural resources.

Improved Environmental Management Planning:

Planning early for tourism development could help in reducing mistakes. It can help in avoiding the gradual deterioration of environmental assets significant to tourism. Green building using energyefficient and nonpolluting construction materials, sewage systems and energy sources is an increasingly important way for the tourism industry to decrease its impact on the environment. Pollution prevention and waste minimization techniques are especially important for the tourism industry.

Environmental Awareness Rising: The tourism industry can play a key role in providing environmental information and raising awareness among tourists of the environmental consequences of their actions.

Protection and Preservation: Several wildlife resources have enacted strict laws protecting animals that draw nature loving tourists. As a result of this, endangered species have thrived again.

Regulatory Measures: Regulatory measures i.e. control the number of tourist activities and movement of visitors within protected area, could help maintain the integrity and validity of the site. Limits should be established through an in-depth analysis and long-term planning. Local cultures and traditions should be taken into account and attempt should be made to promote local ownership and management of programmes and projects. Tourist traffic should be limited according to the carrying capacity of the region. Environmental Impact Assessment (EIA) and Environmental Audits could be a possible legal mechanism of such a plan. Awareness programs and tourist sensitization of the local socio-economic environments should be undertaken.

VI

Travel Agency and Tour Operation

CONCEPT OF TRAVEL AGENCY AND TOUR OPERATION

A travel agent is person or organisation which organises and sells travel like air, railway ticket, transport and accommodation to a tourist. Moreover, a travel agent is a form of business that sells travel related products and services, particularly package tour to the tourists on behalf of travel suppliers such as airline, hotels, tour operator, cruise liners and other travel vendors. In addition to dealing with ordinary tourists most travel agents (depending on organisation) have a special department devoted to travel arrangements/ services for business travellers, while some agencies specialize in commercial and business travellers. Some agencies also serve as general service agents for foreign travel companies in different countries.

The travel agent is one of the most important person in the tourism industry, playing a significant and crucial role in the entire process of conceiving idea and promoting tourism product. In fact, a travel agent packages and processes all core components of a product \ service and present them to the tourists on behalf of travel vendors. In this way it converts a country's attractions, accessibilities, amenities into saleable commodities. Thus, the place of a travel agent is very prominent among the other types of intermediary operations involved in the provisioning and selling of travel products and travel services.

Travel agent/ travel agency is defined as an individual, a firm or company who makes arrangements on behalf of tourists in respect of travel tickets, travel documents-VISA, transportation, accommodation, entertainment, insurance, foreign currency and other travel services from the principal suppliers and sells to the prospective tourists. Thus, the definition clearly identifies that a travel agent/ travel agency is a business may be small or big that sells travel related products and services to end-user customers on behalf of third party travel suppliers/ vendors, such as airlines, hotels and cruise lines. Generally, the clients of travel agencies include tourists and business travellers.

Tour Operator: The term tour operator is used to define the large scale operation in the travel intermediary's process. Thus, 'tour operators' can be wholesaler, and or retailer 5 depending upon market size and organizational structure. Thomas Cook, Thomson, American Express, Cox & Kings, Kuoni, Thomas Bennett are good examples of a dual travel organization. In the Indian tour operation market most tour operators are the outgrowth of successful retail travel agencies in their own travel markets.

A Tour operator is defined as an organization/ firm/ company who package the travel to and from a destination along with complete ground services like accommodation, local sightseeing, local cultural fairs / festivals etc. Interestingly, they provide these services themselves as some of the ingredients of tour package they their own or they arrange these ingredients from different destination operators. Generally, the industry practices indicates that a tour operator is a firm /company which specializes in the developing, planning and actual operation of pre-paid, pre-planned holidays and makes these available for tourists either directly or through the middlemen.When we arrange travel services/ product by own definitely this is a time consuming process. On the other hand there are many people who don't want to bother themselves about arranging, planning and organizing their own journeys rather they want this to done by someone professional expertise. It is the tour operator who packages all attractions of a destination into one composite product and retails it through the travel agents or directly to the tourists. He creates the demand, travel, market and image of the destination. Today, many tourists buy these package tours as per their interests, priorities and budget at a price that is pre-determined. The complete holiday package tour includes travels (air/surface), accommodation, sightseeing, insurance, currency, escort/guide and so on.

The person who puts together all these aspects into a package is known as the Tour Operator. Practically, a tour operator is a firm/ company who provides travel information, plans, organises and coordinates travel related services/ products with various ground operators to create a tour package. At the same time tour operator also ensures smooth conduct and operation of the package tour due to this professional work a tour operator is also called a Tour/Travel consultant or Tour Coordinator. The tour Operator may or may not necessarily have any product of his own but act as an intermediary for different travel vendors to tailor a package to meet the varied needs of a traveller. In fact, a tour operator plays a pivotal role in organizing, explorations, research expeditions, planning and operation a tour package.

Travel Agent and Tour Operator

Historically, the tour operator has mostly emerged from retail travel agency. However, today a clear distinction must be made between a travel agency and a tour operator. Essentially a travel agent is a retailer and tour operator is a wholesaler. The travel agent is a retailer because he sells the travel services to the final consumers i.e. the tourists directly. But unlike the travel agency, the tour operator is a manufacturer of the tourism product. He plans, organises, sells and conducts the tours.He acts as a wholesaler also sometimes because he has to engage travel agents as middleman to sell his package tours in different territories.

The main difference are Travel agents usually sell to end-users on behalf of travel vendors. · Tour operators plan almost each and everything related with tour package. · Tour operators are specialized in dealing with specially one country/ one destination at a time. But there's no specialization in the case of a travel agent. · Most of the cases some travel agents work directly with tour operators and provide the tour operators with the information of clients. · Travel agent gets permit to work from the respective tour operator either private or public while tour operator acquires license from the Ministry of Tourism. · Becoming a travel agent doesn't require so much time/ money as compared to the tour operator. · Tour operator is directly responsible to the regulatory authorities while travel agent is first responsible to the clients and then to the tour operator. · The main source of income of travel agent is commission and other reserves while a tour operator earned profit by providing services/ products to the clients and he also earned commission from the different travel vendors like hoteliers, transporters, airlines, cruise companies and destination companies

The travel agency sector is an important part of the tourism industry but frequently overlooked by the scholars. Most of the studies indicate that travel agencies have become a pivotal aspect and have a profound impact in the growth and development of tourism industry.

A travel agency is defined as an individual, a firm or company who makes arrangements on behalf of tourists in respect of travel tickets, travel documents-VISA, transportation, accommodation, entertainment, insurance, foreign currency and other travel services from the principal suppliers and sells to the prospective tourists. The continuing role and influence of travel agencies should not be underestimated, particularly the pivotal position they occupy within the tourism system. Moreover, to cope with the changing tourism industry market environment numerous travel agencies have been emerging in the tourism market place such as independent , MNCs, retail , whole sale , online , outbound travel agency, handling agency, niche travel agency , mass travel agency

Various types of travel agencies

The Travel agencies are classified on the following basis:

On the basis of distribution chain

According to the International Institute for the Unification of Private law (UNIDROIT), a travel agency can be of two categories. ·

An Intermediary Travel Agency: This type of travel agency undertakes as intermediary to act for another, in obtaining either a journey or a sojourn possible in return for the price for the services. · An Organizing Travel Agency: An organizing Travel Agency undertakes to organize for the public, a journey or sojourn comprising a series of services.

On the basis of Functions

· Retail Travel agency: Retailing mean to sell in small quantity of product / service to the end users. Retailing refers to all the transactions which involve sale of goods or services to the ultimate consumers. A retail travel agency is a middleman between producers and tourists who procures goods from the producers /wholesalers and sells it to the final consumers. They form a vital link in the channel of distribution of products/ services because without travel agency the products/ services would not sell nor would it is possible for consumers to buy services of their choice. They have a much stronger personal relationship with the consumers and deal directly with the people of varied tastes and temperaments.

· Wholesale Travel agency: As the name indicates, a wholesale travel agency operates at large scale and deals in bulk purchase of products/ services and retail through the retail travel agency. Wholesaler may be defined as the middleman who operates between the producers (from whom they purchase goods) and the retailers (to whom they sell goods). Wholesaler refers to any individual or business firm selling goods/ services in relatively large quantities to buyers (retailers) other than the ultimate consumers. Thus, the producers who sell their products directly to retailers may also be regarded as wholesalers. The specialized knowledge and skill of wholesalers increase the efficiency of the distribution network. The wholesalers provide important services and solve the problems of both the manufacturers and the retailers.

On the basis of Tourism flows:

Travel agencies can be categories on the basis of tourism flow such as:

· Outbound Travel Agency: The outbound travel agencies are those travel agencies which provide product and services to tourists want to visit abroad. Generally, these travel agencies provide convenient location for the purchase of travel product/ service besides offering expert product knowledge and ancillary services.

· Handling Travel Agency / Inbound Travel Agency: This is very old form of travel agency which is specialized at a particular destination or location. This travel agency plans and executes of travel packages at destination level. In fact, a handling travel agency represents tour operators at a destination and supervises the delivery of local suppliers.

On the basis of Business or leisure Travel agencies can be categories on the basis of business or leisure such as:

· Leisure Travel Agency: These types of travel agencies manly serve holidaymakers with package tours.

· Business Travel agency: Today, business travel has become core area for many travel agencies. Business travel agency arrange travel for business travelers and corporations and provide extra services such as reporting and travel management.

On Basis of Level of specialization

· Niche Travel agency: Due to the emergence of new form of tourism like ecotourism, Niche travel agencies have evolved. Niche travel agencies and usually small independent travel agencies and specialized in certain products or certain suppliers.

· Mass Travel agency: Mass travel agencies are big travel agencies often large scale/ multinational travel companies. These travel agencies generally offer wide range of destinations and products/services having large supplier network. These travel agencies operate on economies of scale.

Concept of Hospitality

Hospitality aims at providing required service to the guests in which room, food and drinks are mainly included. Accommodation is very important factor for tourism whenever tourist goes outside he/she requires room to stay overnight and needs all other things like food, drink, and entertainment.

Significances of Hospitality Industry

· It generates employment · It generates income · It helps to get foreign exchange earnings · It develops diversification

. **Characteristics/Nature of Hospitality Services**

· Intangibility - Services are impossible to touch and taste

· Perishability - Services of hospitality Industry are Intangible and cannot be stored anywhere that is why if rooms remain empty for a day means it is a loss forever.

· Heterogeneity - Service delivery is always difficult to be same as before and it always varies with each delivery. It is very difficult to standardize its quality.

· Inseparability - Once the services are delivered and it has to be consumed immediately. This cannot be separated as the places of production and consumption like manufacturing goods are same.

· Simultaneity – Production and consumption of the tourism services always happen simultaneously

Tourism is an activity which is run by movement of tourists between destinations for leisure, pleasure, or for business purpose. Tourism is very important for the economy; as it helps in destination development apart from generating employment and providing host of socio-economic benefits. There are many types of tourism such as; mass, alternative, social, religious, adventure, ethnic, historical tourism based on varied criteria. 5 A's and basic components of tourism such as; accommodation, accessibility, amenities, attraction, activity, local, tourist, Infrastructure, information, governance and build environment are considered to be parameters that helps in understanding tourist systems and functions.

VII

Travel Organizations

TRAVEL ORGANIZATIONS

Introduction.

International Travel, Tourism and Hospitality organizations play a major role in advancing the development through the interests of the industry. They provide forums for discussions of common issues, lobby for industry causes, especially those which promote the industry's interests, and allow members from different parts of the world to network and learn from one another. Nearly all organizations are involved in doing research, providing marketing services and training schemes that are most cost effective when done jointly under an umbrella organization.

International Organizations

a. The World Tourism Organization (UNWTO)

The United Nations agency responsible for the promotion of responsible, sustainable and universally accessible tourism. As the leading international organization in the field of tourism, UNWTO promotes tourism as a driver of economic growth, inclusive development and environmental sustainability and offers leadership and support to the sector in advancing knowledge and tourism policies worldwide. The UNWTO encourages the implementation of the Global Code of Ethics for Tourism, to maximize tourism's socio-economic contribution while minimizing its possible negative impacts, and is committed to promote tourism as an instrument in achieving the Sustainable Development Goals (SDGs), geared towards reducing poverty and fostering sustainable development worldwide.

The mission of is to maximise the inclusive and sustainable growth potential of the Travel & Tourism sector by partnering with governments, destinations, communities, and other stakeholders to drive economic development, create jobs, reduce poverty and foster peace, security, and understanding in our world.To realize the Management Vision,

UNWTO's work is based around five distinct pillars:

1. making tourism smarter through celebrating innovation and leading the digital transformation of the sector;

2. making tourism more competitive at every level through promoting investment and promoting entrepreneurship;

3. creating more and better jobs and providing relevant training;

4. building resilience and promoting safe and seamless travel;

5. Harnessing tourism's unique potential to protect cultural and natural heritage and to support communities both economically and socially.

Functioning of UNWTO.

The Secretariat is led by Secretary-General who supervises about 110 full-time staff at UNWTO's Madrid Headquarters. The General Assembly is the principal gathering of the World Tourism Organization. It meets every two years to approve the budget and programme of work and to debate topics of vital importance to the tourism sector.

The UNWTO has six regional commissions-Africa, the Americas, East Asia and the Pacific, Europe, the Middle East and South Asia.

WTO functions thrrough 5 bodies

1.General Assembly

2.Executive Council

3.Regional Commission

4.Committes

5.The Secretariate

WTO has three categories of membership

1.Full members

2.Associate Membership

3.Attiliate Membership

WTO is able to provide assistance in the following areas

* Inventories of existing and potential tourism resources,national tourism development master plan,formulation of policies,plans and programmes for development of domestic tourism

* Safety of Tourist and Tourist facilities

*Training,Feasibility studies for Tourism

*Area development,Development of new tourism sites,development of particular tourism products

*Tourist accommodation planning and operating assistance and hotel classification systems

* Co-operation for development

*Regional activities

*Tourism and Technology

*Quality and Ethics

*Sustainable development

*Market Intelligence

*Communication

The Executive Council is UNWTO's governing board, responsible for ensuring that the Organization carries out its work and adheres to its budget. As host country of UNWTO´s Headquarters, Spain has a permanent seat on the Executive Council. Specialized committees of UNWTO Members advise on management and programme content. These include: the Programme and Budget Committee, the Committee on Statistics and the Tourism Satellite Account, the Committee on Tourism and Competitiveness, the Committee on Tourism and Sustainability, the World Committee on Tourism Ethics and the Committee for the Review of Applications for Affiliate Membership.

b. World Travel and Tourism Council (WTTC).

The World Travel and Tourism Council(WTTC) is a body representing private sectors in all parts of Travel and Tourism Industry and a forum for global business leaders..The mission of WTTC is to maximize the inclusive and sustainable growth potential of the Travel & Tourism sector by partnering with governments, destinations, communities, and other stakeholders to drive economic development, create jobs, reduce poverty and foster peace, security, and understanding in our world.The mission of is to maximise the inclusive and sustainable growth potential of the Travel & Tourism sector by partnering with governments, destinations, communities, and other stakeholders to drive economic development, create jobs, reduce poverty and foster peace, security, and understanding in our world.

WTTC provides an important example of business leaders spending time and money to move their global activity forward while playing a pivotal role in ensuring sustainable development in our ever-changing world.WTTC's research, which quantifies the direct and total impact of Travel & Tourism on our economies in terms of GDP and employment growth has helped to raise awareness of the economic contribution of our industry and continues to feature heavily in the media and in Governments.

c. IATA -International Air Transport Association

It is a world association of scheduled airlines with which they coordinate their efforts to serve their passengers,share their experience and analyse their problems.Its main headquarters are situated at Montreal,Canada.

The aims of IATA are

To promote safe,regular,and economical air transport for the benefit of the peoples of the world, to foster air commerce and to study the problems of airlines

To provide means for colloboration among air transport enterprises engaged directly or indirectly or indirectly in international air transport service

To cooperate with International Civil Aviation Organization (ICAO) and other international organizations.

The major six departments of IATA

a.Traffic department

b.Legal department

c.Technical department

d.Government and Industry affairs department

e.Public relations department

IATA services

1.The global planning of international time table for airline services

2.Maintaining single formula for ticket and airway bills

3.International coordination of telecommunication networks and computer systems

4.Provide training for travel agents and freight agents and undertake various educational programs

5.Examine and solve the problems raised by tourism

d.Pacafic Asia Travel Association (PATA)

Founded in 1951, the Pacific Asia Travel Association (PATA) is a non-profit membership-based association that acts as a catalyst for the responsible development of travel and tourism to, from and within the Asia Pacific region.

PATA facilitates meaningful partnerships to enhance the value, quality and sustainable growth of travel and tourism to, from and within the Asia Pacific region.

The Association provides aligned advocacy, insightful research and innovative events to its member organisations, which including government, state and city tourism bodies; international airlines and airports; hospitality organisations, and educational institutions, as well as thousands of young tourism professional (YTP) members across the world.

The PATA network also embraces the grassroots activism the PATA Chapters and Student Chapters, who organise numerous travel industry training programmes and business development events across the world.

The main objectives of PATA are:

• To promote and develop tourism in the Pacific region. • To provide timely up-to-date and informed. • To organize seminars/ conferences for the members. • Build the business of members. • To organize training and development programs for members. • To promote ethical practices. • To focus on destination development. • To take the lead position on travel and tourism industry issues that need to be addressed. • To stimulate and develop public-private sector partnerships. • To improve international understanding and international corporation. • To provide a common forum. • To publish material relating the tourism industry. • HR development. • Marketing research and statics. • To provide valuable insights, forecasts, and analysis help members to make better business decisions.

PATA Membership

The membership of the PATA is open to all organizations which contribute in the travel and tourism sector directly and indirectly. Generally, the membership of PATA is open to all professional organizations such as airlines, steamship lines, travel agencies, tour operators, hoteliers, government, tourism professional organizations, advertising agencies, and public relations agencies, etc. Roles and Functions of PATA Generally, PATA's main aim is the progressive development and promotion of tourism to its member countries.

The contribution, role, and functions of PATA towards its members can be studied under the following points:

• PATA conducts research studies on tourism. • PATA organizes marketing programs. • Provides detailed and up-to-date information. • Organize events in the Pacific region. • Helps in economic development. • PATA helps in the improvement of tourist plants and service facilities.

e) International Civil Aviation Organization (ICAO).

The International Civil Aviation Organization (ICAO) is a UN specialized agency, established by States in 1944 to manage the administration and governance of the Convention on International Civil Aviation (Chicago Convention). ICAO works with the Convention's 191 Member States and industry groups to reach consensus on international civil aviation Standards and Recommended Practices (SARPs) and policies in support of a safe, efficient, secure, economically sustainable and environmentally responsible civil aviation sector.

ICAO also coordinates assistance and capacity building for States in support of numerous aviation development objectives; produces global plans to coordinate multilateral strategic progress for safety and air navigation; monitors and reports on numerous air transport sector performance metrics; and audits States' civil aviation oversight capabilities in the areas of safety and security.

ICAO develops policies and Standards, undertakes compliance audits, performs studies and analyses, provides assistance and builds aviation capacity through many other activities and the cooperation of its Member States and stakeholders.

f) United Federations of Travel Agents' Associations (UFTAA).

Universal Federation of Travel Agents 'Associations (UFTAA) was formed on November 22nd 1966 in Rome. . As a globally recognized body UFTAA is the longest established negotiating partner with the leading travel and tourism organizations in the world. Of a special importance is the close co-operation with IATA, representing the interest of individual travel agents and as a partner in the IATA-UFTAA Training Programme. Two other organizations with close relationship are the International Hotel and Restaurant Association (IH&RA) and the International Road Union (IRU). UFTAA is needed more than ever before to defend and promote the interests of travel agencies in their professional work on behalf and for the travelling consumers.UFTAA offers to its membership the valuable opportunity to be involved with UFTAA's networking global platform in order to support good health of travel and tourism industry. UFTAA encourages associations; organizations; institutions and individual member agencies in Travel, Tourism and Hospitality industry to get connected .

Functions of UFTAA.

To comply with its mission, the Confederation develops the following functions: · To unite and consolidate the Federations of Travel Agents' National Associations and to globally enhance the interests of their members · To represent the travel agents' activities before various worldwide bodies, governmental authorities and suppliers · To work towards the adoption of measures that will ease travel for the consumer and to offer services to its member federations · To offer, as a voluntary mechanism, an arbitration service which assists in solving conflicts resulting from commercial relations for which amicable settlement cannot be reached · To organize a world congress of travel agents and other meetings necessary to the exchange and transmission of knowledge.

NATIONAL ORGANISATIONS

a) Indian Tourism Development Corporation(ITDC)

The India Tourism Development Corporation (**ITDC**) is a hospitality, retail and education company owned by Government of India, under Ministry of Tourism. Established in 1966, it owns over 17 properties under the Ashok Group of Hotels brand, across India.

Objectives of ITDC

Establishment and management of tourist transport facilities. .

Providing consultancy services and training for tourism-related projects.

Promote tourism traffic in the country through food festivals, fairs and joint ventures abroad.

Organise cultural and entertainment programmes.

Functions of India Tourism Development Corporation (ITDC)

To construct, take over and manage existing hotels and market hotels, Beach Resorts, Travellers' Lodges/Restaurants;

- To provide transport, entertainment, shopping and conventional services;
- To produce, distribute, tourist publicity material;
- To render consultancy-cum-managerial services in India and abroad;
- To carry on the business as Full-Fledged Money Changers (FFMC), restricted money changers etc;
- To provide innovating, dependable and value for money solutions to the needs of tourism development and engineering industry including providing consultancy and project implementation.

The Corporation is running hotels, restaurants at various places for tourists, besides providing transport facilities. In addition, the Corporation is engaged in production, distribution and sale of tourist publicity literature and providing entertainment and duty free shopping facilities to the tourists. The Corporation has diversified into new avenues/innovative services like Full-Fledged Money Changer (FFMC) services, engineering related consultancy services etc. The Ashok Institute of Hospitality & Tourism Management of the Corporation imparts training and education in the field of Tourism and Hospitality.

ITDC has a network of Ashok Group of Hotels, Joint Venture Hotels, Restaurants (including one Airport Restaurant), Transport Units, Tourist Service Station, Duty Free Shops at International as well as Domestic Customs Airports,

b)Directorate General of Civil Aviation (DGCA)

The Directorate General of Civil Aviation (DGCA) is the regulatory body in the field of Civil Aviation, primarily dealing with safety issues. It is responsible for regulation of air transport services to/from/within India and for enforcement of civil air regulations, air safety, and airworthiness standards. The DGCA also co-ordinates all regulatory functions with the International Civil Aviation Organisation (ICAO).

Functions of DGCA:

Formulation of standards of airworthiness for civil aircraft registered in India and grant of certificates of airworthiness to such aircraft.

Promoting indigenous design and manufacture of aircraft and aircraft components by acting as a catalytic agent.

Indian aviation industry is dominated by private airlines and these include low cost carriers, who have made air travel affordable.

- Licensing of pilots, aircraft maintenance engineers and flight engineers, and conducting examinations and checks for that purpose.
- Licensing of air traffic controllers.
- Certification of aerodromes and CNS/ATM facilities.
- Granting of Air Operator's Certificates to Indian carriers and regulation of air transport services operating to/from/within/over India by Indian and foreign operators, including clearance of scheduled and non-scheduled flights of such operators.
- Conducting investigation into accidents/incidents and taking accident prevention measures including formulation of implementation of Safety Aviation Management programmes.
- Carrying out amendments to the Aircraft Act, the Aircraft Rules and the Civil Aviation Requirements for complying with the amendments to ICAO Annexes, and initiating proposals for amendment to any other

Act or for passing a new Act in order to give effect to an international Convention or amendment to an existing Convention.

- Coordination at national level for flexi-use of air space by civil and military air traffic agencies and interaction with ICAO for provision of more air routes for civil use through Indian air space.
- Keeping a check on aircraft noise and engine emissions in accordance with ICAO Annex 16 and collaborating with the environmental authorities in this matter, if required.
- Promoting indigenous design and manufacture of aircraft and aircraft components by acting as a catalytic agent.
- Approving training programmes of operators for carriage of dangerous goods, issuing authorizations for carriage of dangerous goods, etc

c)Airports Authority of India, or AAI,

The Airports Authority of India, or AAI, is a public sector enterprise under the ownership of the Ministry of Civil Aviation, Government of India.

It is responsible for creating, upgrading, maintaining, and managing civil aviation infrastructure in India. It provides Communication Navigation Surveillance/Air Traffic Management (CNS/ATM) services over the Indian airspace and adjoining oceanic areas. AAI currently manages a total of 137airports, including 34international airports, 10 Customs Airports, 81 domestic airports, and 23 Civil enclaves at Defense airfields.

Founded in 1995, the Airports Authority of India was created through the Airports Authority of India Act, 1994 under the aegis of the Ministry of Civil Aviation. Hence, it is a statutory body.

- The AAI manages the building, enhancing, servicing and management of the civil aviation infrastructure in India.
- The major function of the AAI is to provide Air Traffic Management (ATM) services over airspaces that belong to the Indian Territory and the neighbouring oceanic areas.
- It also provides CNS (Communication Navigation Surveillance).
- It is responsible for the creation, management, maintenance and up-gradation of aviation infrastructure in the country. Management of international airports, domestic airports, customs airports and civil enclaves in the defence airfields is vested in the AAI.
- The headquarters of the Airports Authority of India is in New Delhi.

AAI was formed with the responsibility of building, enhancing, managing and servicing the infrastructure for civil aviation in India. Providing Air Traffic Management services over airspaces is one of the main functions of AAI.

d).The Archaeological Survey of India (ASI)

The Archaeological Survey of India (ASI), under the Ministry of Culture, was established in the year 1861 is the premier organization for the archaeological researches and protection of the cultural heritage of the nation. Users can get detailed information related to excavations, conservations, museums, epigraphical studies, etc.

The Archaeological Survey of India or ASI is an attached agency of the Ministry of Culture of the Government of India.

- It engages in archaeological research and conservation, and protection and preservation of ancient monuments and archaeological sites in the country.
- ASI regulates all archaeological activities conducted in the country through the provisions of the Ancient Monuments and Archaeological Sites and Remains Act (AMASR Act), 1958.
- It also regulates the Antiquities and Art Treasure Act, 1972.

It was founded in 1861 by a British Army engineer who took a keen interest in archaeology in India, James Cunningham.Archaeological pursuits started much earlier, in the 18th century, when Sir William Jones formed the Asiatic Society in 1784 together with a group of antiquarians.Alexander Cunnigham is also known as the 'Father of Indian Archaeology'.It is astatutory body after independence, under the AMASR Act, 1958.ASI is headed by a Director-General and is headquartered in New Delhi.It has more than 3500 protected monuments and archaeological sites of National Importance that it protects and preserves.

e) Indian Association of Tour Operators (IATO)

The Indian Association of Tour Operators (IATO) was founded in the year 1982.The main objectives are to promote global peace and goodwill. It is a united travel forum that promotes and supports the growth of tourism in India. The members consist of all tourism-related industries. It has over 1600 to its members. The members participate during national distress and national emergencies. It also works towards the growth and expansion of the tourism industry. It provides a forum for discussions and meetings with other tourism-related providers for promotion.

f)Tourism Finance Corporation of India (TFCI)

It is an India-based financial institution. The Company provides financial assistance for new, expansion, diversification, renovation/modernization projects in the tourism sector, services sector and related activities, facilities and services.Established as a premier tourism financing institution, TFCI has acted as a catalyst in creation of infrastructure in hospitality segment in over 3 decades of its existence. TFCI has also enabled various businesses to channelize their investments into different segments and locations of the tourism industry.

Tourism Finance Corporation of India was incorporated as a public limited company under the Company Act, 1956 on 27th January 1989. The operational activities were started on 1st February 1989. It was set up as a specialized cell to cater to the needs of Tourism and Hotel Industry. It was expected to ensure priority in funding tourism and tourism-related projects. The organizational structure of TFCI is consisting of the board of directors, managing directors and other professional staff at middle and lower levels. Theoretically, the board of directors is a supreme organ of the management of TFCI. The organizational structure of TFCI is consisting of the board of directors, managing directors and other professional staff at middle and lower levels.

The main functions of TFCI

To commence and carry on the business of assisting industrial, commercial, professional and trading enterprises – corporate bodies, partnership firms, trust, individuals or other concern whosoever constituted and engaged or to be engaged in setting up and development of tourism, hotel, and tourism-related activities.

To commence and carry on the business of lending or granting by way of loans or advances in rupees and/or foreign currency or in any other form money with or without interest or with or without security for the purpose of assisting enterprises in India.

1. To commence and carry on the business of facilitating, through the grant of loans and other financial, technical and professional assistance, the acquisition, maintenance, modification, construction, reconstruction, refurbishing and renovation of tourism and travel related activities.

2. To commence and carry on the activities of coordinating and formulating guidelines and policies relating to the financing of all such

projects in the tourism and tourism-related activities, facilities and services.

3. To commence and carry on the development and promotional functions with regard to tourism and tourism-related activities.
4. To commence and carry on the business of merchant banking and other allied activities.
5. To commence and carry on the business as assessors, designers, draftsman, estimators, surveyors and other materials.
6. To commence and carry on or be interested in the business of buying, selling, distributing, leasing, exporting and importing of furniture, machinery, equipment, and other material.
7. To carry on business as share brokers and agents of insurance for all kinds and for all of the risks.
8. To carry on the business of agents for the central or state government or any other international or national institution or organization in the transaction of any business concerned with tourism and tourism-related activities, facilities and services.

g) IRCTC(Indian Railway Catering and Tourism Corporation)

Indian Railway Catering and Tourism Corporation Ltd. has been set up by the Ministry of Railways with the basic purpose of hiving off entire catering and tourism activity of the railways to the new Corporation so as to professionalize and upgrade these services with public-private participation.

The Indian Railway Catering and Tourism Corporation Limited (IRCTC) is a public sector enterprise under the Ministry of Railways, Government of India. IRCTC was established on 27th September 1999 as an apex body of Indian railway to cater and manage hospitality on railway stations and trains to promote Indian tourism at domestic as well as international level.

IRCTC headquarter is situated into the heart of national capital New Delhi. To operate the operations smoothly five zonal offices are working in Delhi, Kolkata, Mumbai, Chennai & Secunderabad. IRCTC provides complete travel and tourism solutions for the various customer segments and also catering to trains and at stations over the Indian Railway network. It is also called "Lifeline of the nation".

IRCTC provides the following range of products and services:

Luxury Tourist Trains

Exclusive steam and hill charters

Chartering of special trains and coaches over the Indian Railway network.

Tour packages – Bharat Darshan – special tourist trains for the budget traveler.

Hotels – near important railways station all over India.

Car rentals

E-ticketing for travel over Indian Railways

Call centers – for rail and tourism related information.

Onboard catering on trains all over the Indian Railway network.

Multi-cuisine food plazas at important railway stations.

Packaged drinking water – Rail Neer

Buddhist circuit special train

Tatkal Scheme facility

With the availability of such wide range of services under one umbrella, IRCTC is, thus, able to offer readymade as well as customized packages to meet the requirement of all segments of the travel and tourism industry.

Luxury Tourist Trains

IRCTC works with Indian Railway and other public and private organizations in the tourism sector, for running of luxury trains over the Indian Railways network. These include Palace on Wheels, Deccan Odyssey, Heritage in Wheels, and Fairy Queen.

h) Indian Association of Tour Operators(IATO)

The main role of IATO is: · To promote national integration, international welfare and goodwill · To take necessary steps for promotion, encouragements and development of tourism in the country 9 · To develop, promote and encourage friendly feelings among the tour operators and travel agents/agencies · To protect the interest of the members · To setup and maintain high ethical standards. · To settle the disputes of the members. · To communicate and negotiate with chambers of commerce, · To get affiliation with tourism organisations in other countries. · To organise promotional tours with DoT, Airlines and International Tourism bodies. · To institute awards for excellence in travel trade. · Protect the members from the mal-practices · Provides information. · Assists tourism educational institutions to shape their students as per industry requirements · Provide well quality of Human resources · Promote ethical and sustainable operational / managerial practices

Kerala Tourism Development Corporation (KTDC)

KTDC is a public sector that conducts and regulates the tourism activities in the Indian state of Kerala. The KTDC is headquartered at Trivandrum and has offices across all the districts. The agency also operates hotels, resorts, and tourist rest houses in key locations in the state. Its official slogan is "Official host to God's own country." It is one of the most profitable ventures of the Kerala government.It is a public sector that conducts and regulates the tourism activities in Kerala. The agency also operates hotels, resorts, and tourist rest houses in key locations in the state . Objectives of KTDC

- To promote Kerala as a leading tourist destination
- To identify key tourist destinations within Kerala and promote it outside
- To provide auxiliary support in developing key tourist destinations
- To provide highest quality hospitality services to tourists
- To act as one-source destination for various informations regarding tourist destinations and other related informations.
- To ensure higher returns to government, through financial and social viable projects, and thereby provide employment
- KTDC owns 3 flagship properties known for its historical importance.
- Bolgatty Resort in Kochi, which houses the Bolgatty Palace, a heritage property which is the largest Dutch palace. Built in 1635 as Palace of Dutch Governor of India, this soon became British Residency for Travancore-Cochin Kingdoms. The palace is part of Bolgatty resort which has another property, branded as Island Resort, which has a nine-course golf club, horsing tracks and other facilities.
- Mascot Hotel at Trivandrum, located in state capital Thiruvananthapuram is a heritage property built in 1902 which used to accommodate Travancore Army officials and Army Center until 1949.
- Lake Palace, a former summer palace of the King of Travancore, is on an island in the middle of the Periyar Lake — 20 minutes by boat from the mainland, located inside the Periyar Tiger Reserve.

KTDC also provides various packages to different tourist destinations.The hotels and resorts are of various budgets.A speciality of KTDC properties is that they provide their guest with a unique tourist experience.

The National Tourist Organisation (NTO)

NTO is the body responsible for the formulation and implementation of national tourist policy. It is the proper agency and instrument for the execution of the national government's responsibilities for the control, direction and promotion of tourism.

- All countries which are engaged in tourism have a national tourism organisation which plays a leading role in both the formulation and the implementation of the government's tourism programme.
- This organisation is also responsible for coordinating the different activities of all the bodies interested in tourism development. The national tourist organisation may be a full- fledged ministry, a directorate general, a department, corporation or board.

Functions of N T O:

The objectives of a National Tourist Organisation are to ensure that the maximum possible value from international tourism accrues to the country for its economic and social benefit. To achieve this objective, the N T O has three main functions which are Research,Information and promotion within the country,,Regularisation of standards of lodging and restaurants, Control of activities of private travel agencies, Publicity overseas,Technical and juridical problems, International relations, Development of select areas and Overall tourism policy and promotion.

Research is a basic function of a national tourist organisation. A concomitant of institutional promotion is research into the tourism potential of the principal markets and investigation into the marketability of the country's tourist product. This is an important direct responsibility of the NTO.

Information and promotion within the country helps not only the actual international tourist but also, the domestic tourist. The information offices located at important tourist centres serve as a facility to the tourist. These are a major aid to tourists both overseas as well as local.

These centres provide important and accurate up-to-date information to tourists visiting various places. In most countries, the NTO has its own branch offices in strategic places throughout the country. These offices are responsible for information and reception service for visitors and liaison with the local tourist interests.

It is also the responsibility of the N T O to encourage and promote tourism consciousness among the government agencies and the public so that they will realise the benefits that a country can derive from tourism. Regularisation of standards lodging and restaurants is very essential for tourist satisfaction.

Since the growth of tourism depends directly on consumer satisfaction, the N T O is its role of administrator, manager and promoter of tourist product, acts as the government watchdog to ensure the maintenance of appropriate standards of quality and service of lodging establishments.

This supervisory role has been enlarged and strengthened because of the complex problem arising from the growth of tourism and the expanding needs for safeguarding the interest of tourists. The degree of tourism development, and of the travel sector's maturity, naturally determines the extent to which the travel industries are self-regulating and the scope of the N T O's supervisory role.

Control of activities of private travel agencies is another important supervisory role of the NTO. More and more tourists are utilising the service of private travel agencies. It is essential that the tourist should get good and efficient service and protection.

The NTO should be responsible for the maintenance of appropriate standards of quality and service of the travel agents. Travel agents should be regarded as having professional's status and this could best be brought about by introducing appropriate legislation of the NTO. One of the most important activities of any national tourist office is promotion of the country as a destination for tourists.

Among other activities, promotion includes advertising, publicity of all kinds, public relations, the provision of information and the distribution of printed sales material. Planned publicity and promotion on behalf of the country are among the basic functions common to all N T Os.

The NTOs cooperate with other governmental departments and the travel trade in promoting tourism for their country.

Technical and Juridical problems are those which are related with the administration of law. This is very crucial as on it will depend the quality of various services provided by various sectors. N T Os have to be very cautious while, administering law. Technical problems on the other hand are concerned with the development and maintenance of various services.

Continuous detailed assessment has to be made of the extent to which the infrastructure, superstructure and organisation plans are likely to meet future tourism demands. It is imperative that the N T O should take part directly in each of these stages.

The optimum development of tourism in any country implies a close knowledge of the attractions of the market: the processing and presentation of the country's attractions in the manner most favourable and acceptable to the market; action of the market to create effective demands; and the provision of adequate facilities, amenities and service to ensure the maximum satisfaction of tourists. All these areas are of u technical nature and the NTOs have to take proper care for their efficient maintenance.

International relations are a very essential part of tourism. International contacts resulting from tourism have always been among the most important ways of spreading ideas about other cultures. Tourism can be a vehicle for international understanding by way of bringing diverse people face to face.

It is the responsibility of the NTO to deal with those aspects of tourism development that have a bearing on relations with foreign countries.

It maintains offices and representatives abroad for the promotion of tourism traffic to the country, and has close relations with foreign tour operators, travel agents and carriers. It cooperates with NTOs of neighbouring countries in mounting joint regional travel promotion programmes.

Governments also empower NTOs to represent the country's tourism interests in international organisations and, wherever necessary, to join with other government agencies in negotiations for the conclusion of agreements in the field of tourism with foreign governments.

Development of selected areas to attract tourists is necessary. In every country there are hundreds of areas of tourist's potential. However, due to various constraints, it is not possible to develop all these areas. It is important to identify and select certain areas which have the maximum potential for tourism development.

A detailed scientific survey of these areas will help in avoiding wasteful expenditure. To the extent permitted by its economic resources, the NTOs should encourage development of selected resorts.

Existing possibilities of attracting tourists for mountaineering, winter spots, beaches, national parks, pilgrim centres, folk traditions and customs, festivals and sporting events-should likewise be developed and protected.

The National Tourist Organisation in a developing country should consider obtaining a preliminary survey in clearly what positive tourist attractions existed and how they could most effectively be developed within the limits of the resource available.

Overall tourism policy and promotion are very essential as they help in the optimum utilisation of resources. In calculating returns from investments in tourism, the national tourist policy cannot restrict itself to limited considerations of immediate financial and economic profitability.

It has to consider the beneficial effects of tourism on general national development where consideration of non-economic character may be equally or even more important than purely economic returns, viz, cultural considerations, social consideration, political consideration, etc.

The NTOs should take all these factors into consideration while formulating overall tourism policy and promotion. The NTOs should not consider tourism from its balance of payments aspects alone, but should take into account contribution which tourism makes to international trade by developing the national economy and enhancing social values.

The Organisation and Work of the NTO

The National Tourist Organisation is likely to be concerned with the following four broad areas:

(i) Administration, (it) Production, (iii) Marketing and (iv) Financing

The administration will be concerned with the personnel of the organisation, with the part to be played by tourism in the overall national development plan, with effective liaison with concerned government departments like finance, home, planning, health, transport, communications, education, culture, public works, labour .etc. Regional cooperation and legal matters and advisory service etc.

The production part will be concerned with all those elements and activities which make up the tourism product. Production will include the inventory and assessment of the country's natural attractions and the development and protection of these assets; the requirements in infrastructure where tourist development is to be planned.The marketing areas will be concerned with research into the principal and potential tourist markets, their size, socio economic characteristics, preferences of tourists for food and accommodation, spending power and the like, with sales promotion, public relations, advertising, maintenance of overeats offices, etc. and collaboration with other countries in the same region.

Destination Management Organizations (DMOs) are the backbone of tourism destinations. They exist to promote destinations, attract visitors, and develop a regional economy. DMOs are responsible for everything from attracting major sporting events to promoting local festivals. They work with businesses to help them understand what travelers need to have an enjoyable experience

Successful DMOs and destination managers play an essential role in managing tourism at the local level to help attract tourists and support businesses within its boundaries. They're also responsible for promoting it through positioning statements, branding campaigns, high-quality product development, effective communication with stakeholders (e.g., residents), and maximizing financial resources available from both public and private sources, while ensuring value for money spent on projects that meet overall objectives.

DMOs engage in a variety of activities that will help promote and develop sustainable travel practices, including:

- Educating travelers about the destination's attractions and offerings
- Marketing through targeted campaigns
- Working with other organizations on issues related to sustainability to achieve common goals
- Addressing resident concerns related to tourism

CONTENT

Tourism: Concept and Definition, History of tourism :(India & World), Ancient, Medieval and Modern history -Factors influencing the growth of tourism- Multi-disciplinary aspect of tourism –Tourism classification: inbound and outbound tourism-international and domestic-intraregional and inter regional. Tourism: Benefits and Impacts-An overview.Motivation – Definition –Travel Motivation-Physical, Cultural, Interpersonal and status and prestige, with relevant examples and further divisions – Health, Rest, Recreation, Relaxation. Wander lust and sun lust-Plog's theory of tourism motivation- Maslow's theory of motivation and tourism-Career opportunities in tourism industry – International travel requirements (Passport, Visa, and Health Certificates & Insurance).Tourism Demand – Demand Meaning, Definition, Measurement of Tourism Demand, Determinants of Tourism Demand- Indicators of Tourism Demand of a population -Measuring Demand for Tourism- Problems of measuring tourism demand-Tourist Statistics – Types of tourist statistics: Volume, value and visitor profile– Methods of measurement – Problems – satellite tourism account – meaning Tourism industry–components (5A'sAttraction, Accessibility, Accommodation, Amenities and Activities), Tourism system and Elements (Leeper's Model) – Tourism industry: the concept-Characteristics of Tourism (Intangibility, Perishability, Variability,

Inseparability, Heterogeneous, Multitude of industry, pricing competitiveness/Flexibility, Interrelationship of elements. Role of government in tourism: NTO and DMO- Industrial elements: principals and intermediaries-Travel Agent-Tour Operator-Transportation: Various modes of transport-Accommodation and Hospitality,Tourism organizations: Classification and purposes- International- Objectives and functions of UNWTO, IATA, WTTC, PATA- National Tourism Organizations: Objectives and functions of ITDC, DGCA, AAI, ASI, IRCTC, TFCI, IATO, Regional: Kerala Tourism Development Corporation (KTDC) Activities and functions

Model Questions

Section A

Answer all question each question carries 2 marks(Short answer type, not to exceed 50 words each)

1. Define Tourism

2. Write the major benefits of Tourism

3. What is cultural motivation?

4. Name the Tourism Minister in the Union Ministry

5. Give the major classification of Tourism

6. What is a passport?

7. What is the basic need according to Maslow's theory?

8. List any two indicators of Tourism Demand

9. Define Amenities

10. Why Tourism Products are said to be inseparable?

11. Who is a Tour Operator?

12. Give the role of NTO's in Tourism Development

13. Expand IATA. Give any two functional bodies of IATA

14. Which organization is the official host of Kerala Tourism?

15. Write short note on IATO

Section B

Answer 6 questions. Each question carries 5 marks.(Paragraph / Problem type, not to exceed 100 words each)

16. Give an account of Grand Tour Period

17. Why Romans are called the first pleasure travellers

18. Write a short note on Travel motivation

19. Distinguish between sun lust and wanderlust

20. Describe Leiper's model of Tourism System
21. Write a note on water transportation
22. Discuss the functions of WTTC
23.Describe the need of Organizations in Tourism Industry

Section C

Answer any two Questions. Each question carries 10 marks.(Essay type, not to exceed 500 words)

24. Write an essay on the history of development of Tourism in India
25. Explain the various methods of measuring Tourism demand
26. Describe the objectives and functions of ITDC
27. Give a brief account of the A's in Tourism **(2x10=20 marks)**

ॐ

ॐ

VIII